The Desire to Write

Graeme Harper

The Desire to Write

The Five Keys to Creative Writing

© Graeme Harper, under exclusive licence to Springer Nature Limited 2019

All rights reserved. No reproduction, copy or transmission of this publication may be made without written permission.

No portion of this publication may be reproduced, copied or transmitted save with written permission or in accordance with the provisions of the Copyright, Designs and Patents Act 1988, or under the terms of any licence permitting limited copying issued by the Copyright Licensing Agency, Saffron House, 6–10 Kirby Street, London EC1N 8TS.

Any person who does any unauthorized act in relation to this publication may be liable to criminal prosecution and civil claims for damages.

The author has asserted his right to be identified as the author of this work in accordance with the Copyright, Designs and Patents Act 1988.

First published 2019 by
RED GLOBE PRESS

Red Globe Press in the UK is an imprint of Springer Nature Limited, registered in England, company number 785998, of 4 Crinan Street, London N1 9XW.

Red Globe Press® is a registered trademark in the United States, the United Kingdom, Europe and other countries.

ISBN 978–1–137–51991–7 hardback
ISBN 978–1–137–51990–0 paperback

This book is printed on paper suitable for recycling and made from fully managed and sustained forest sources. Logging, pulping and manufacturing processes are expected to conform to the environmental regulations of the country of origin.

A catalogue record for this book is available from the British Library.

A catalog record for this book is available from the Library of Congress.

Contents

Preface		vii
Introduction: So You Want to be a Creative Writer?		ix
1	Intention	1
2	Action	27
3	Emotion	51
4	Imagination	71
5	Pleasure	95
Conclusion: Being a Creative Writer		115
Notes		125
Index		129

Preface

Graeme Harper is a Professor of Creative Writing and Dean of The Honors College at Oakland University in Michigan, USA. An award-winning fiction writer, and former Commonwealth scholar in Creative Writing, he has published widely on Creative Writing. He was awarded the first doctorate in Creative Writing in Australia (from the University of Technology, Sydney). He holds a second doctorate in Creative and Critical Writing from the well-known University of East Anglia program in the United Kingdom. From 2008 to 2011, he was inaugural Chair of Higher Education at the UK's National Association of Writers in Education (NAWE). Today he is a member of the Executive Board and Chair of Research at the Creative Writing Studies Organization (CWSO) in the USA and Editor-in-Chief of the journal *New Writing: The*

International Journal for the Practice and Theory of Creative Writing. He is also Founder/Director of the Great Writing International Creative Writing Conference. His latest work of fiction is *The Japanese Cook* (2018).

Introduction

So You Want to be a Creative Writer?

No single story explains the desire to be a creative writer. Your story, your own individual desire to do some creative writing, will be distinctive, will draw on your life experiences, and will be empowered by your personal belief in creative writing providing you with a positive experience. Perhaps it is your love of language, and creative writing giving you the freedom to engage in it, that draws you to being a writer. Perhaps it is the writing puzzles that creative writing poses and you need to solve. Perhaps your primary motivation is intellectual, or visceral, or expressive, or evidentiary. The word 'desire' refers to a strength of feeling and it is used here to emphasize that without a strength of feeling very little creative writing ever gets done, and almost never is it sustained. That is, desire relates directly to your motivation, your willingness to act. Writers naturally have varying levels of motivation, more or less willingness to act at specific times and in general; but a desire to write is always the key force needed to become a creative writer and to remain a creative writer. With this in mind, it might be more than coincidence that human desire is also regularly the subject of a creative writer's explorations.

'In my experience,' writes American novelist, Jane Smiley, winner of the Pulitzer Prize for Fiction for *A Thousand Acres* (1991), 'there is only one motivation, and that is desire. No reasons or principle contain it or stand against it' (Humphreys, 1989: 1). In *The Marriage of Heaven and Hell* (1790), William Blake, the eighteenth-century English poet and artist, writes that 'those who restrain desire do so because theirs is weak enough to be restrained'. Desire involves our emotions and it involves our reasoning. In this we draw upon both our intellect (our understanding) and our imagination (our ability to project mental representations of something not currently observable, not immediately accessible to the senses). To illustrate the different stories of creative writers, here are three examples, two short and one longer:

The School Student

A boy stands up in a class of around twenty students. These are kids of 14–15 years of age. This is a school in North Wales, UK, so these are children in what has been called Key Stage 4, Year 10, in UK high school education. I am visiting to talk to them about creative writing, perhaps introduce a few writing exercises. My visit is all entirely informal, simply the result of a casual invitation from an interested English Language teacher. So there's no fixed program of activities. The students in the room have elected to attend my visit rather than stay in their English class. They have also been encouraged to do so by their English teacher. So, they're both self-selecting and selected, in a way I seem to recall things in high school sometimes seem to work.

As an icebreaker, I have just asked the group if anyone already does any writing. The standing boy, now holding up sheets of paper he's pulled from his backpack, begins to read out a story he's written about a dystopian future where the seas have risen to cover much of the land.

The Patient

I am in what was once called Yugoslavia, somewhere southeast of the city of Novi Sad, I think. I can't be sure. It was dark for much of the journey here. It is 1990, not too long before the constituent republics of the Socialist Federal Republic of Yugoslavia will begin to break apart. It is a warm June, but it is a cool early evening, so there is a light fog descending in the area, because though the day has been warm here there is the colder evening air above deep lakes and in dark forests. The small villages we have seen, dimly lit, thatched and stony like those you might picture if asked to recall early modern Europe, have been left behind. The bus we are on turned into a narrow private road some time back, and we moved through stands of trees into an increasingly dark expanse. For ten or fifteen minutes we seemed no longer in anywhere at all, just in the dark, and the animated private conversation of our two Yugoslavian hosts, who appear to be boyfriend and girlfriend, added no further information. However, we had been told, earlier, that we were visiting a government facility. There are twelve other writers with me, from such countries as Japan, Poland, Italy, China, Portugal, Romania. Just a moment ago, the narrow roadway swung open into a circular drive and in front of us now is a building which even the least romantic among us can only consider a castle.

The bus stopping in front of the long stone steps, the arched doorway, stone lions on pedestals either side of us. We are invited by our bus hosts to step out. There are people emerging from the castle. They are mostly in white coats, so I immediately think this must be some kind of medical facility. This makes a degree of sense, but there is a certain lack of intention about their appearance. They seem like relatives who have been waiting a while for us to visit. It dawns on me this castle has no other signs suggesting it deals in medical issues. In fact, it has no signs of any kind, no directional indicators of anything like wards or radiography or oncology, nothing like that. Other than the white coats, these could simply be our aunts and uncles who live in a castle in the Yugoslavian countryside and are coming out to greet us.

We are eagerly guided by our hosts, up the steps. Inside, the walls of the castle are an aqua color and seem more from the mid-twentieth-century history than ancient history. There are corridors ahead of us, that meet at checkpoints, where men in white uniforms sit at small wooden tables. The castle dwellers, more enthusiastic than ever now, are urging us down the initial corridor, and though they are not speaking, assuming quite rightly that none of our group other than our bus hosts speaks Serbo-Croat, they are explaining something somehow. Somehow, they seem to be saying (or indicating, more accurately) that what we have come for is right ahead of us. That when we reach whatever it is that is ahead we will have reached our destination and, in the way of journeys to somewhere and for something, we will be satisfied, perhaps even pleased.

We turn once, and then again, the corridors now painted white rather than aqua, and then we are abruptly on a ramp that leads into a large room. The room is wide and its ceilings are low, and ahead of us and all around the room there are white painted bench seats, dozens of them, at odd angles. In the center of the room, which has one windowed wall, but it is dark so we can't see out, there is open area with a mosaic pattern in dark blue and turquoise and lime-green tiles. The area is slightly recessed into the floor and there is a large square drain hole in the center, as if whatever happens there is regularly washed away.

The white-coated greeters are gesturing for us to come down the ramp and to take seats on the benches. As we do so, one of them is heading back down the corridor. While we wait, our bus hosts, who are speaking now in whispers, come around to each of us and explain in their strong but heavily accented English that this is a facility for medical therapies of many kinds and that the patients here have been told of our visit and in our honor they would like to do something for us. We each show delight at this, but at the same time it's obvious that several in our group are unsure what a gathering of patients might entail, what such a gathering might entail specifically here in Yugoslavia, and, given that there is now no option to choose not to be honored, how they should react. Doubling this sense of delighted unease, not one of us speaks the language that is now being spoken, and spoken more energetically and more loudly all around us. Largely no one in the group speaks each other's first language very well either, though we make do with broken conversations in various configurations of English, each entering these conversations now with a sense of trans-linguistic solidarity.

From down the corridor the white-coated doctor, who appears to be in charge of much that is going on in this castle, reappears, striding. Proudly he proceeds down the ramp. He stamps his shoes when he reaches the floor of the room. Then he turns back up the ramp and gestures toward those who are now approaching it. We can make out more white-coated folks. But they are mingling now with some other folks, and whether anyone would admit it or not, it is these new folks every one of our group is watching. Other than the absence of white coats, they at first seem no different to anyone else. Indeed, that is the impression that sticks with me most throughout the whole visit, that lingers in interesting ways for some hours, days, and ultimately, to be frank, years afterward.

We're not given much chance to make further observations. The coat-less group is directed toward a collection of the white benches to the right of us, and at a short distance away. Then the doctor in charge steps into the center of the mosaic circle and, with the assistance of our male bus host (our female bus host seated up front, attentively watching proceedings) welcomes us to his hospital and sincerely compliments us all on our work, which I'm fairly sure he could not know but which he engages with in such a way that I can't but help feel appreciated. At that point, in what clearly appears to have been a predetermined plan, one of the patients is invited to come to the center of the mosaic. She all but sprints to the task. Briefly introduced, simply by name, as T_____ the doctor is quickly retiring from the circle, as is our bus host, leaving T_____ there now on her own.

Standing over the drain hole, and not yet acknowledging us, T_____ reaches into the pocket of her gray cardigan. From it she brings out several small scraps of paper. Not one of the pieces is the same size as another, and because of this, in her hands, they appear like a handful of leaves. She looks up at us now, smiling a little but doing nothing else. Suddenly, from the wings, the doctor starts explaining, in very broken English, that T_____ had been very excited when she heard of our impending visit, knowing our eminence and so forth, and that she is a creative writer too. T_____ seems both proud to have this acknowledged and somewhat daunted by it too. But the doctor and our male bus host are urging her to perform and after three or four passages of urging, some of which sound quite ardent, she begins to read from her scraps.

For almost forty minutes we sat, and occasionally applauded, while T_____, who was a young woman of maybe twenty-three or twenty-four, read what was apparently poetry, in a language none of us understood, about what we therefore had no idea. She did so in a careful, quiet way – none of the exuberance you might see in a rendition of performance poetry, and none of the reverence you often hear in a reading of poetry designed for the page. She read with a humbleness that had her turning to the doctor after every few lines for confirmation, and he in turn shaking his hand at her, a gesture meaning 'continue'. She read, it seemed, not only on her own behalf but on the behalf of the other patients and staff who, because of this, energetically applauded her after every poem, as did we. Some of the patients it seemed, with their expressions distant and detached, were not entirely in the room; a few were in wheelchairs; one leant awkwardly against one of the pillars in the room, rubbing his forehead against it.

She read not only from each piece of paper but around it, turning each small piece over in a pattern of reading that was uninterrupted, despite its tortuous journey. Many of the poems were apparently about her experiences in the castle, where she had been for three years now. A few of the poems were about animals, pets, that she had once owned in childhood and remembered vividly. One poem was apparently about our impending visit, and I still wish that I had asked someone, one of our bus hosts, to translate it so that I could understand where we figured in her life, and how she imagined we'd come about being there and what it was that our being there in that remote Yugoslavian hospital was doing for her.

The Professor

Recently let us say, to create some immediacy for this final story, though it actually occurred a handful of years ago, I arrived at an American university to take up a new administrative position. Every change of institution and location, every new role has both fueled excitement and made some demands. This change was doing that, but more so. Having worked in various parts of the world, including nearly a quarter of century of short-term appointments in the USA, my new role meant a relocation from the United Kingdom to the USA for some time, perhaps even permanently. That alone was simultaneously energizing and challenging.

I knew no one at my new institution, other than those on the Search Committee for the position and some of the university's senior administrators, to whom I was only introduced during two days of interviews. The university was not one I had ever visited, prior to my interview. I knew little about the State it was in, and even less about the university's surrounding area. Although I kept much of this to myself the Search Committee Chair, an energetic senior professor happily heading toward retirement, kindly paid particular attention to settling my family and me. He made numerous introductions, and arranged a couple of social gatherings at his home so my family and I could meet faculty, the current and the retired. Even in the American system of making university appointments, which in my experience tends to be more holistic and more comprehensive than those in other parts of the world, as Search Chair he went above and beyond.

About a week into arriving, and apparently encouraged by the Search Chair, a professor in a discipline that was not Creative Writing got in contact to ask if I would like to meet for coffee. The context was that he too had moved internationally. It was a generous and pleasant email exchange, and so we met up – and had an equally pleasant meeting. The topical thing is what happened next.

The next day, and although the subject of my own disciplinary interests had not come up at our meeting, an email arrived from the professor with a tentative request. His email was in part a follow-up from earlier, checking in, generously inquiring if all was okay given we were barely arrived, that kind of thing. Then a question. He said he had been working on writing a novel for a while, just something he liked to do between his own academic activities, and wondered if I had time to take a look at some of it. He wasn't sure whether it was any good, though he wrote other things for work purposes, of course, and quite a number of them had been accepted for publication in noted academic journals. However, he wasn't sure exactly what he might do with this, the results of his creative writing. But there it was nevertheless, this part of his life, something he did in his leisure time, but also something that felt like it had some connection with his disciplinary explorations, his traveling, his way of interpreting the world, his sense of self.

For those who like closure in their stories: I guessed the Search Chair had mentioned something about my interests, and that prompted the professor's inquiry; and I did agree to read some of his novel-in-progress. In my view, not half bad! I made a few suggestions. I don't know if he ever finished the work or did anything more at all with it.

What's Your Story?

I chose the stories of the high school student, the hospital patient, and the university professor (in Anthropology, as it happens) from a considerable number of other encounters with fellow creative writers to show that circumstances and individual motivation inform the desire to write creatively. Other factors certainly play a role: education, familiarity with your chosen genre of writing, encouragement from teachers, family or friends, a love of words. But whatever influences or impacts on you, it will be the existence and persistence of a desire to write creatively that will be the clue to whether you become a creative writer, develop further as a creative writer, and continue to be a creative writer.

The high school student, the hospital patient, and the university professor each was undertaking creative writing without being *required* to do so. They wrote out of class, off the job, and not because they were told or even encouraged to do it. Each one of them simply *wanted* to write creatively. They were personally moved to do so. Each made an individual decision, informed by their environment (the language learning of high school, the therapeutic conditions of a hospital, the writing cultures prevalent in higher education), but nevertheless determined not primarily by those environmental conditions or by any perceived requirements, but by their singular, individual *desire* to undertake creative writing, to employ creative writing for some purpose, to invest time and effort in writing creatively, with the aim that they each would gain some kind of satisfaction.

None of these facts asks us for our value judgments on the end products of your writing. None of them can be approached very successfully if we begin with the idea that we all undertake creative writing for exactly the same reasons. In other words, while the description 'creative writer' is an occupational category, and largely one that became fortified in the modern period, the period influenced by the Industrial Revolution (that is, from the late eighteenth century) when occupational categories increasingly became ways of defining our economic roles, the term is not a judgment of the value of you undertaking some creative writing, nor should it negate or gloss your individuality in deference to an occupational category or a sweeping definition of what is done and what is achieved when you personally write creatively.

Similarly, the question here is not whether the hospital patient's poetry was more accomplished than the professor's novel or the professor's novel better than the high school student's short story. When we think of creative writing from the point of view of the *undertaking* of it, we're referring to an activity not only the results of an activity. So this is not a case of using the words 'creative writing' to describe a physical object like a novel or a poem or a screenplay, though such an object might indeed be part of your desire to write.

There are five key aspects of creative writing. Each contributes to your desire to do it, and each informs how you can understand and develop your writing, the things you do, and the material results of you doing them. In plain language, your desire to engage in creative writing is as simple as you concluding that 'I want/need/would like to express myself through creative writing', and then going ahead and doing so. A combination of this simple statement and the concepts that underpin it reveals a great deal about the practice of creative writing and a great deal about you as a writer as well, whether a beginning creative writer or an experienced one.

The five keys to creative writing, directly related to your desire to undertake it and key parts of your personal story, are:

1. Intention
2. Action
3. Emotion
4. Imagination
5. Pleasure

If you come to understand these five keys to your creative writing, grasp them as they relate to your writing, explore their qualities, and master their influence, you not only come to understand your own desire to write but explore and examine the basis of creative writing itself, your own and that of other creative writers. In doing so, you will have a clearer sense of why it is that you have a desire to be a creative writer and of what sustains you or will sustain you as a creative writer.

What follows is an examination of each of the five keys, individually, though they are in reality in constant and dynamic communication with each other. That fluidity of communication is significant in emphasizing that creative writing always works by associations and relationships – such aspects as content, structure, subject, theme, all equally having roles in the practice and in its results. Being attentive to the five keys – intention, action, emotion, imagination, and pleasure – will provide you with productive guidance whatever type, genre, or form of creative writing you undertake.

1

Intention

Asking that Big Question

At what we might call the 'big question' level of creative writing, the level at which you make the personal decision to do some writing, you have deemed to put other things you have to do or like to do aside, to take the time, find the place, employ whatever equipment you need (laptop, pencil, phone), do whatever you can to set forth or to continue with creative writing. You have expressed a macro intention or intentions. This means that your state of mind concerned with writing, your holistic mindset, anticipates that you will act in a certain way.

There might not be an easy or effective method of dividing your holistic mental state into smaller components. In fact, it might be that your determination to do some creative writing is comprised of many integrated parts, a number of which are not easily accessible to you. Such a suggestion has informed approaches to creativity throughout history where the mystery of why and how creativity happens has encouraged commentators to suggest creativity is largely critically inaccessible to us; or, at the very least, that we can understand only some elements of it.

Other elements are said to be transcendental, that is, they are beyond ordinary human experience. What this idea encompasses is inclusive of your emotions, your intellect, and your imagination. There is an interaction and an integration in creative practice of these complex elements. Add to this your choice to intentionally make your writing creative and the answer to the big question, the macro element of your decision making and your determination, is connected to a particular form of human endeavor, an identifiable artistic practice and a distinctive mode of communication.

There are clearly cause and effect associations, one thing following another, in your decision to become a creative writer. Associations also in that you have certain expectations about your creative writing, and about your experience of doing it. Your sense of the experience your creative writing will provide for you is associated with your natural desire for the predominance of pleasure over pain – in the simplest terms, that is. In short, your intention has several dimensions, connected with your feelings, your intellect, and your imagination. We can hear something of that melding of feeling, thought, critical thinking, and imaginative empowerment in the words of Neil Gaiman, whose works include comic books and graphic novels, films, novels, and more, perhaps even something of his intention, when he writes in *Fragile Things: Short Fictions and Wonders*:

> Stories like people and butterflies and songbirds' eggs, and human hearts and dreams, are also fragile things, made up

of nothing stronger or more lasting than twenty-six letters and a handful of punctuation marks. Or they are words on the air, composed of sounds and ideas – abstract, invisible, gone once they've been spoken – and what could be more frail than that? But some stories, small, simple ones about setting out on adventure or people doing wonders, tales of miracles and monsters, have outlasted all the people who told them, and some of them have outlasted the lands in which they were created. (Gaiman, 2007: xxxxii)

Fragile beauty and yet, potentially, robust longevity, Gaiman suggests – clearly, in his description, something that attracts him to being a creative writer.

Can you write creatively, unintentionally? Undoubtedly! But in that instance creativity, which is most frequently viewed as a positive element in our lives, an ingenious contribution to various human practices, could instead be seen as a negative. Think here of the work-related email that is too offbeat or too whimsical, or the technical report that is too fanciful. The suggestion in those instances that your writing is 'creative' would not be a compliment but a criticism.

The macro level of engagement with creative writing involves your intentions. This macro, or proposition, level is where you are making the decision to actually *do* some creative writing not just talk about doing it, perhaps dealing with what that doing will mean for your daily life, considering how to put your decision into play, what steps to take, exploring what you know about creative writing generally, perhaps what you know broadly about the form and genre you're attracted to writing. At this macro level, your intentions involve:

Commitment – This means a decision made, some emotional engagement, a tacit or explicit promise to yourself.

It does not yet mean action. Intention is not in itself *doing* writing. But it does mean striking an agreement with yourself, one that you aim not to break. The term 'commitment' also suggests writing involves a degree of labor. How much labor is involved varies greatly between creative writers and between projects, and although there are suggested well-worn measures of effort in creative writing (for example, the notion that a novel is according to its length alone a big effort) there is actually no absolute or proven correlation between how much effort you apply and how successfully you reach your creative writing goals. Certainly it would be simpler, and perhaps even more ethically satisfying, if there was a creative writing commitment equation along the lines of Amount of Effort × Length of Effort = Amount of Success. It is common to hear suggestions akin to this equation. For example, 'creative writing is hard work; it involves a large amount of conscious editing, and it takes place over long periods of time with frequent revisions' (Sawyer, 175). Perhaps, sometimes. But the general truth about amounts of effort involved lies elsewhere. Knowledge about creative writing plays a role, an affinity for a particular genre, psychological traits such as the ability to live with uncertainty and flexibility and self-confidence. Commitment is a component of intention, not a measure of your potential for success in creative writing.

Planning – This might involve some outward expression of your intention. For example, you might tell a partner, family, or friend that you will be unavailable at a certain time (you might or might not openly declare that you'll be writing). You might physically begin planning a story, a novel, a screenplay, jotting down notes or ideas for a poem or play. More likely than any of this, the first signs of your intentions will be expressed by your internal rather than external planning. Internal planning is significant because creative writing is not only its physical evidence (drafts, emails to a publisher or editor, completed works); it is also your thinking, emotional engagement, speculating, imagining. Internal planning is not necessarily before a physical act of writing; it can also occur multiple times during your writing actions. In fact, over the period of composing a work while your decision to undertake some creative writing is maintained, and in being so is supported by your physical actions of writing, your internal planning might be altered, impacted upon by conditions experienced during the composition of the work, by your changing thoughts and emotions, and even just simply by the logistics of getting from the beginning of writing a work to the end of writing one.

Reasoning – Being emotionally committed to undertaking creative writing relates to your personal belief in creative writing as a form of expression, as a method of exploring and presenting not only information (which indeed might not benefit in other writing circumstances from the influence of the imagination and of creativity) but also your feelings. Nevertheless, writing is a type of human communication that involves the organized use of words, which are units of language that carry a meaning.

So emotion, part of your proposition, your macro decision to be a creative writer, is also attached to written language as a significant component of human interaction that symbolizes and communicates. Creative writing is not therefore entirely an outpouring of emotion; it is also a concerted organizing of communicative and symbolic elements. To do that organizing, your writing involves reasoning. Your intentions involve reasoning about the choice to write creatively, and they involve comparative reasoning about choosing creative writing over other modes of art and other modes of communication. Along the way, in the composing of a work, your reasoning also influences your choice of the tools of language that you use and how you use those tools.

Perception – When you decide to undertake some creative writing you also address questions of perception. Your perceptions of creative writing and about the results of such writing, how you regard these and how you understand these, your mental image of these things. Perception involves your interpretation of sensory information. So, your experience of having seen or heard works of creative writing – even the physical sensation of writing, or the look and feel of physical objects associated with creative writing, such as books – influence your intention. Perception also relates to what can be called 'normalizing', whereby you have a set of activities you would regard as a 'normal' part of your life, or which you perceive can be introduced into your life. Intention at this macro level also relates to social and cultural norms, contexts through which you navigate the world. We come to understand social situations because we develop a set of interpretative understandings of what other people are doing, what they want, how they might behave. With this in mind, your own intention of undertaking creative writing will also relate to the intentions you perceive in other people.

At your decision point, that proposition level of creative writing where you answer that big question 'Will I be a creative writer?', your desire to write is connected to your belief that your commitment, reasoned progress, and truth of perception about the experience and results of your creative writing will ultimately bring you some form of satisfaction. Taking a moment or two to consider this provides you with a practical, interpretative tool for understanding your decision to be a creative writer and for examining how that desire to write creatively impacts on your actions that follow.

Compositional Questions

Your affirmation that you will undertake some creative writing is the framework into which your other writerly actions all fit. These writerly actions are at what we can call the micro level of individual action, day-to-day writing decision making, compositional querying. That is, while intention clearly influences your decision making at the macro level, it is also something with which you as a creative writer work regularly when composing a work. After all, such writing involves your reasoned action. Creative writing is a specific kind of writing, with specific characteristics and specific results, so accidental creative writing is writing that was meant for another purpose and is unlikely to be successful for that planned purpose. Imaginative, reasoned, in numerous ways planned, and applied creative writing based on your perceptions – this is the basis of your intention to be a creative writer or to continue to undertake some creative writing. You make a decision to write creatively and you animate, maintain, and nurture this – that is the definition of being a creative writer.

As there is a larger framework for your desire to write creatively, so within that framework are intentions that will be displayed in your micro level thoughts and actions. More extensively, your intentions will influence your reasons for creating individual works of a particular type, in a particular genre and of a particular form, your methods and patterns of creating (which could include your choice of a place to create and of an instrument with which to create).

Type, Genre, Form

Type, genre, and form are words sometimes used interchangeably by commentators. These three words will be used here in a specific way. **Type** here refers to works with common written characteristics (for example, poetry, screenplay, novel). **Genre** in this instance means a category, works of creative writing with agreed inter-type conventions (for example, comedy, horror, tragedy, science fiction, romance; some observers also define fiction and nonfiction as core genres, and that too is the convention suggested here). Genre or categorical definitions shift over time and are open to cultural influence and interpretation as well. **Form** here is referring to the organization of a work, its construction. You could therefore be working on a novel (type) that is a comedy (genre) presented in letters (form).

Type

Your choice of what type of writing you engage in can be well explored from the point of view of attraction and of satisfaction. In essence, you favor a certain type of creative writing because it attracts you and promises you your preferred form of satisfaction. Choice of type could be said to work at both a micro level (that is, influencing individual compositional action) and at the macro level (that is, how you envisage your writing, are motivated to do it, project an end result of doing it). Here there is something of a moment of truth.

Imagine that while you are enchanted by poetry, as an art form, as a mode of communication, that you might even consider the challenge of writing poetry to be a writing challenge above all others, you nevertheless intend to write a screenplay. The reason for your intention is simple enough. While you admire the writing of poetry, the end results of poetry writing, the physical object that is a poem, generally speaking the entire artistic and communicative contributions to humanity of poets and of poetry, your intention in your creative writing is to write something that brings you financial reward and you do not believe writing poetry will ever do that. Given our media versus literary consumption habits in the contemporary world, that is probably a fair assessment.

The elements of your choosing of particular type of writing are complex but accessible. Your choice is likely first informed by your awareness and admiration. This does not mean that you necessarily have an extensive experience or knowledge of that particular type of creative writing. Simply, that you are aware of its existence, most likely have felt and appreciated its influence, and that you are prepared to act upon your interest. Your perception, reasoning, commitment, and some preliminary internal planning inform your choice, and your choice informs your intention. You might not have yet written anything of the type you are intending to write, but you have experienced that type of creative writing as reader or audience. As reader or audience, you are able to relate examples of this particular type of writing, perhaps both those you admire and those you find wanting, and you might have considered how genre and form interact with this type of creative writing.

Your intention in choosing a particular type of writing, by the simple logic of knowing the type in some way, is to reproduce the type you have experienced. In other words, if we take type to represent works with common characteristics then, in order to produce a type of creative writing, your intention is to map your own writing on to what you have identified as those typological conventions. Of course, if you have only experienced a type of creative writing as reader or audience not as a writer, then it is likely you do not have a developed sense of what the actual writing of that type of such writing involves or sometimes even of how a final work appears. Two good examples of this are the screenplay and the libretto.

In the case of the screenplay and the libretto, the writing type defined by the final work does not give you knowledge of how either of these two are produced, or how they might appear in their final written form. This is because both of these creative writing types act as guides for another art form, film in the former instance and opera in the latter. You can work backward from the finished work to the type of creative writing behind it, but in that sense you are beginning where the work is completed, and attempting to reconstruct the creating of the work without access to observed or reported evidence of how it was and is actually done.

If your attraction to a certain type of writing is defined in the first instance by the satisfaction you gain from the finished product that in itself is not clear-cut evidence that you will gain satisfaction from undertaking that type of creative writing. So, for example, if you get considerable satisfaction from *reading* a novel this is not evidence you will gain any satisfaction from *writing* a novel. Here we see the difference in type between defining creative writing as its final physical appearance and defining creative writing as the actions of writing creatively. The former might be the way in which you first encounter evidence of a type of creative writing, probably where you first come to admire a type of such writing, but it is not in itself the actions of writing, the actual practice of creative writing.

Your intentions in relation to types of creative writing therefore raise important questions about your desire to be a creative writer. That desire, which is a strength of feeling directly related to your motivation and willingness to take action, gains from one or more of the following:

Exposure to the experiences of other creative writers, and particularly (though not solely) those working on similar types of writing. That exposure might be through direct observation of those writers writing, but much more often it will be via such things as reading autobiographies and biographies of creative writers, or reading their memoirs or interviews with them, or listening to particular writers read and speak at public events. And, of course, it is bolstered (if not completely satisfied) through exposure to their finished works. Mario Vargas Llosa, in his discussion of his love of the works of Jorge Luis Borges, not least relating this to their shared Latin American heritage, calls reading Borges 'a sinful passion', noting that since his youthful discovery of his works that passion has 'never faded'. 'Re-reading him,' Llosa says, 'which I have done from time to time like someone performing a ritual, has always been a happy experience' (Llosa, 1991: 3). Exposure to other writers, endeavoring to ground their final works in stories of their composition, strengthens familiarity with your writing practice, generally; and, given your interest in a particular type of writing, and intention to write that type, it can also provide you with an opportunity for direct experiential knowledge.

Education connected to types of creative writing. Classes with versions of titles such as 'Writing the Novel' or 'Writing Poetry', or 'Writing for Digital Media' highlight specific typological elements. While there are benefits in intersecting discussions between creative writing types – because all such writing uses language and language structures; all such writing imaginatively employs word choice and rhetorical devices; all such writing is by definition seeking to provide inventive, original expression – those classes that focus on specific types of creative writing offer the opportunity for more in-depth exploration of types. Given that in contemporary education these are often incorporated into a program of study involving exposure to multiple types of creative writing, they also give opportunities for making informed practice-based comparisons.

The experience of attempting to write. We hear of the importance of failure in ultimately reaching success. Nevertheless, your desire to write is very unlikely to be your desire to fail. We always find through writing practice those types of creative writing with which we appear to have more success. Failure with other types can of course lead to or support that conclusion. The reasons for your success might include your ability to conceptualize form in certain types of writing but not as much in others, or your confidence in patterns of composition that best support certain results. This is simply to name a couple of examples. There are cognitive reasons for this as well as cultural ones, that is, your individual processes of memory and reasoning and coming to know, as well as the influences of arts and modes of communication that follow particular patterns or present ideas, themes, and subjects in particular ways. Without actually doing some creative writing there is no way of determining the type of creative writing with which you will have most success. What will be successful for you as a creative writer is not wedded either to the levels of your critical understanding or the final results of creative writing. That is why extremely skilled literary critics are not by default always successful novelists or poets. In fact, it is only rarely the case. There is also the significant question of how you define success.

Your definition of success will be incorporated into your intentions. If your intention is to write and illustrate a picture book to entertain the younger members of your family, and ultimately you do that and get that result, it would be spurious to consider that your writing was unsuccessful, based on other expectations. If you write a short story with the intention of winning a particular short story prize and it does not do that, then your intentions have not been met. If you write poetry because you find it assists you expressing ideas and emotions that you do not feel are otherwise satisfied, then your intention has been met and you have been successful.

Types of writing can certainly be delineated according to their physical shape, the manifestation of their common characteristics according to a critical analysis of structure and appearance. But if you begin as a creative writer by thinking of creative writing type from the point of view of your writerly intentions, where you undertake a particular type of writing because you are attracted to it and it provides you with satisfaction, then success is defined by meeting your intentions. This doesn't change the fact that creative writing types refer to common characteristics observable in the completed physical object, that is, say, a novel, a play, a poem. What it does do is focus your attention on undertaking creative writing rather than focus on established final appearances of texts. Such observable types of writing are based on visual, concrete archetypes and their supporting textual paradigms. In essence, this means that the outward appearance of a novel will appear to be that of a novel, and its internal forms and their function will match expectations, however broad these might be, of what it means to be a novel. It is always more conceivable that a creative writer will work toward such typical, observable examples; after all, these are accepted, observable models based on repeated patterns of appearance, usually established over some time. However, creative writing is also imaginative and inventive. In being so, when you begin at the point of your intentions, and you engage with your writerly actions that follow, then your creating of any type of creative writing always has the potential to challenge archetypes and established paradigmatic models. Your experience of writing creatively is in this way both learning the typological conventions to which you are attracted and potentially questioning them, endeavoring to alter them or to recreate them to better suit your intentions.

Genre

Your intention in choosing a genre has origins beyond typological conventions, beyond definitions of type. In the case of genre, your creative writing intentions are associated with your appreciation of particular aesthetics, content, style, and tone. Choice of genre could also be said to work at both micro and macro levels – though in genre's case relating to codes of communication, with both public and personal dimensions.

Your own appreciation of the aesthetics of a genre draws from your sensory responses, whereby you encounter a category of creative writing, a genre, and you respond positively to it. You thus intend to pursue a certain genre of creative writing because your encounter with it brought you pleasure. Simply, the genre made you feel something; you had a physical reaction of which you are either conscious or unconscious – for example, a reaction that is manifest in your laughter at a comedy, or your tears during a touching moment in a drama, or your sense of awe felt in response to a work of science fiction. That reaction has been strong enough that you intend to act on it.

The aesthetics of genre are also more than this. You choose a genre that not only produces a sensory response from you but appeals to your emotions: you are moved by the genre to feel something. Accompanying this, your aesthetic response entails your intellectual judgment. Senses reacting, emotions engaged, you analytically consider the genre – judging that it is apt for the subject or theme, or that it has an exceptional ability to connect ideas and response, or that it is superior in its precision or its depth of investigation or its ability to entertain, or in its associations with the experience of your own life, or that is has value based on cultural, economic, or political conditions that influence your sense of its value.

In addition to subject and theme your intention to write creatively in a particular genre also relates more broadly to content. This is initially based on how you imagine your perceived content will benefit from the recognized conventions of a particular genre. Let's say you intend to write a story with a primary theme concerned with the bonds across humanity, as established in the stumbling discoveries of urban youth, combined with a subject that focuses on a fascinating piece of American history (say, the conditions of postwar industrial Alabama, in the years leading up to the Montgomery Bus Boycott). You envisage this content will best flourish in a drama. You don't envisage this content will best be developed as a work of science fiction or comedy. This choosing of genre has asked for your aesthetic judgment, drawing from your sensory responses, your emotional engagement, and your intellectual analysis. How you see content relating to, or not relating to, a particular genre is directly a result of such judgment, responses, and analysis. Your most productive choice of genre in this way is always based on two primary concepts: 'suitability' and 'fitness for purpose'.

Suitability refers to how you envisage a genre as the container and fosterer of your ideas, your interpretations, your creative arguments, as we might call those viewpoints and opinions you present through creative means. In other words, suitability is your answer to the question: Is this genre likely to support my creative vision? Suitability also has another meaning in referring to cultural perceptions and social mores, whereby topics of exploration are regarded as appropriate for certain genres but not for others. Content and genre in this latter sense are matched based on your individual ethics and on societal beliefs that are historically, culturally, and politically determined – for example, what is suitable for comedy in the twenty-first century in one country might be seen as unsuitable in another or have been unsuitable in the same country at an earlier time. Creative writers' intentions quite simply reflect both their place and their time. This latter sense of suitability is encountered regularly in casual conversations on what is or is not appropriate for certain contemporary audiences – children, for example – as well as subjects and approaches to those subjects that are seen to disregard civility. This social mores definition of suitability is, of course, also formally incorporated into legal systems of censorship.

Fitness for purpose is a measure you can use to determine whether your choice of genre to support your intentions matches not only how that genre is suitable for your creative vision, likely to be appropriate for the content you have in mind, and supports your themes and subjects, but also whether it meets such criteria as appealing to your chosen audience, reaching your goal of recording an event or events previously unrecorded, considering something you have not previously had the opportunity to creatively consider. These are examples of criteria that are part of your intentions. So, while suitability might confirm how a genre supports content, subjects, and themes, and in doing so empowers your creative vision, fitness for purpose is a useful tool for considering a genre's applicability to your other aims.

Your choice of genre, additionally, involves stylistic choices. Such things as your selection of certain words and your structuring of units of language such as sentences and paragraphs. Because creative writing highlights the creative, the imaginative, and the inventive, such stylistic choices are potentially greater or more varied than they are in other forms of writing. In the same diverse way, genre involves choices of tone. Your intentions guide you here as well. In music, tone is often related to timbre, referring to distinctive qualities of sound. In creative writing you might think of tone more as attitude or as the character of a piece of work, that you work to create in the process of composition, and that keeps in play the viewpoint or viewpoints in the piece you are creating. Genre conventions, suitability, and fitness for purpose will shape your stylistic and tonal choices. Ultimately, however, your intentions are your overarching guide to the writing choices you make.

Form

Finally form, used here to refer to your writerly organization of a work of writing and the elements of its construction, is to intention as detail is to observation. That is, the casual observer of an event might miss any number of details much as the less attentive creative writer might treat the use of form in creative writing merely as an extension of having chosen a genre and/or type of writing. While you can choose a type of creative writing and a genre, your intentions cannot really be fully met without your purposeful attention to form. If your decision to undertake some creative writing, or to continue to do so, is a proposition, and genre is a bringing together of the macro and micro dimensions of that choice, then your decisions regarding form could be called an adaptable consequence.

Because creative writing involves your reasoned action, form involves your reasoned action in singular instances and in connected organizational choices – each compositional choice you make, and each compositional choice related to another compositional choice. Knowing creative writing is a specific kind of writing, with specific characteristics and specific results, this can mean your choices favor certain constructional emphases. For example, descriptive writing over expository writing, or narrative writing over persuasive writing; your use of the personal more prevalent than your attention to the overtly informational. However, these are generalizations. Creative writing is inventive and eclectic, so your use of form can be equally as inventive and eclectic. How you navigate the use of form will depend on your ability to reason out how form choices will impact the delivery of your intentions, and then to apply creative writing skills that capitalize on your reasoning.

From the point of view of literary criticism, some might say that the creative writer's choice of form does not necessarily lead to truths about the finished work, or even about what the writer was intending. This is true enough in that when you are writing you are engaging both thoughts and actions that are conscious and those that are unconscious. The unconscious is almost entirely unreachable, though there are those using practices such as psychoanalysis who have long endeavored to reach and understand unconscious mental processes. Literary criticism correctly recognizes the difficulties and complexity of doing this. However, approaching creative writing from a creative writer's point of view, and given that your unconscious is largely unreachable, forms can most productively be regarded as tools chosen by you for a purpose. The primary variations to consider are those that potentially do exist between how you envisage the impact of your choice of form on your chosen reader/audience and how that form might *actually* impact on your chosen reader/audience.

As a creative writer you are so often endeavoring to move between the personal and the public. In other words, it is very unlikely you will have polled your readership and are creating your work based on responses to a survey regarding the impact your decisions will have on that readership. Your reasoning is therefore based on your experience and on speculation, and it is influenced by any education you may have received in creative writing. Questions arise: Do you know all choices of forms at your disposal? Have you applicable technical knowledge of how different writing forms are constructed? Have you considered reported reader/audience responses to particular creative writing forms? These might well have validity and influence your decision making. Is your intention to use a certain form in relatively conventional ways or are you aiming to make one part of your appeal to your reader/audience surprise at how a certain form is used? Consider the use of footnotes in Vladimir Nabokov's novel *Pale Fire* or Mark Z. Danielewski's novel *House of Leaves* – footnotes are a familiar formal component of academic publications, but relatively unfamiliar in novels, and made even more arresting by much fictionalizing of the references in these novels.

Your choices and ultimately your decisions regarding form return again and again to your intentions, to suitability and fitness for purpose based on those intentions, and to how choices of form represent intention at the compositional coalface. Forms vary in themselves, of course, and you can compare and contrast choices of similar forms in the works of other creative writers. For example, how does one screenwriter use descriptive writing compared to the use made of description by another screenwriter? There are no universal rules about descriptive writing in screenplay writing. However, some critical opinion suggests that too much descriptive writing is in effect an example of 'directing on paper' and that adjectival writing in screenplays should therefore be kept to a minimum in order to better recognize the role of the director in directing the production process. Alternative critical opinion sees descriptive writing in the screenplay as an aspect of style and an opportunity to better shape a vision of the imagined final film. Comparing completed screenplays can provide you with evidence of different screenwriters' sense of form. Forms can of course also vary over your writing of one instance or work of creative writing. You might construct a poem with a consistent rhyme pattern, but feel your intentions are best met by moving between narrative and descriptive forms, interspersed with the lyrical. While writing forms involve structure and function, your employment of them is influenced just as much by your imagination and your feelings. Your actions in employing forms will be influenced by personal cognitive forces, how you individually recognize, perceive, and know things. Form in creative writing is therefore both physical organization, often clear by the appearance of your writing on the page or screen, and your personal response to the subjects and themes that you are investigating.

Patterns and Methods of Creating

By defining your intention to be a creative writer you suggest your commitment to the use of your time and environment in certain ways in order to undertake your creative writing. These certain ways are as varied in nature as those of us who choose to be creative writers. Defined by your intention, you perceive, seek out, and create your creative writing habitat or habitats. Of course, not all the mysteries of creative writing are resolved in doing so, and it might be that some of your attraction to being a creative writer comes from trusting in this fact. E.L. Doctorow, author of such works as *The Book of Daniel* (1971), *Ragtime* (1975), *Billy Bathgate* (1989), and *Homer & Langley* (2009) references this. 'Composition is very mysterious,' he says, 'creativity is very mysterious. I think when you're writing at your best, you don't work from calculation, you're not illustrating a preconception. You trust to the act of writing' (Morris, 1999: 35).

While there are a great number of books that suggest habitual commonalities between creative writers – such things as you requiring somewhere quiet to write, or the significance of you having an undisturbed length of writing time – your patterns and methods of creating will best be served by your accurate perception of what best suits you personally. Your creative writing habitat or habitats will be ecological, as are all habitats, related not only to the objects within the habitat but also to interactions that occur there, and to patterns of behavior – yours and those of others. You produce consistencies and continuities in behavior during your time as a creative writer, and you introduce, explore, and pursue variations, perhaps in relation to the launching of work on a new project or the need of a new outlook on one already in motion. In general, some activities and objects will remain fixed for long periods of time, because these elements of your writing habitat are felt to provide fundamental support for your methods of composing, or your ways of thinking, or the empowerment of your imagination. Other activities and objects will be introduced or sought out by you cyclically as you determine where you are in considering ideas, making imaginative leaps, physically attempting to write.

For example, you might generally buy books on a relevant subject at a certain point in your cycle of composition; you might begin composing on the screen or on paper, consistently in an ordered way, favoring one physical method or another; you might expect a certain number of words to be your average per day or per week, simply based on your previous results. These things return cyclically as part of your creative writing habitat. Further still, you will introduce new activities and objects as you seek to create a method of composing a specific work that is located in compositional time and place. No work of writing emerges without spatial and temporal context impacting upon it.

Understanding this guides you toward identifying your patterns and methods of creating that are relatively fixed, those that are cyclical, and those that are new and potentially designed to positively disrupt previous patterns and methods. Intention generates these behaviors and assists in forming and reforming habitats.

Across the patterns of creative writing, you **draft** – that is, create in the first instance or in a way that suggests fluidity and change – you **revise** – that is, return to earlier writing to reconsider, reimagine, recompose, and aim to improve – and you **edit** – that is, prepare work for completion, seek to materially conclude your creative writing in line with your intentions. These patterns of creating, like all aspects of your creative writing habitat, are subject to varying degrees of consistency, continuity, variation, and change. Intention is therefore key to establishing long-term and cyclical behavior that will bring about creative writing. Intention is also key to introducing new behaviors that relate to specific writing projects and that either confirm or disrupt aspects of your writing habitat.

Commitment, planning, reasoning, and perception inform your decision to write creatively – this is the macro. Your intention has several dimensions, connected with your feelings, your intellect, and your imagination. Compositional questions determine your choice of type, genre, and form – this is the micro.

The first signs of your intentions will be expressed by your internal planning. Your patterns and methods of composing, creating, and recreating your habitat, through your actions and your interactions with others and with the society and culture around you, put your intentions into motion. Your desire to write creatively is connected to your belief that your commitment, reasoned progress, and perception about your creative writing will ultimately bring you satisfaction.

Exploring Intention

- Consider your personal definition of success with creative writing, taking into account what will give you satisfaction. This will inform your intentions.
- Creative writing is an identifiable artistic practice and a distinctive mode of communication. Ask why you chose creative writing over other art forms, other methods of communication.
- When assessing what drives and maintains your writing, examine your commitment, planning, reasoning, and perception.
- Apply knowledge of your intentions to how you consider compositional questions, answering why you choose to employ certain types, genre, and forms. This provides you with a creative writing compositional map.
- Your intentions inform all drafting, revising, and editing – effectively guiding these practices.
- Create and recreate your creative writing habitat with your intentions in mind.

2

Action

Inaction

If you do not at some point take action, you will not at some point be a creative writer. No question. Creative writing is, ultimately, your actions. It must be so because at a very basic level writing involves you inscribing something; that is, it involves you literally or figuratively (say, on a computer screen) marking, etching, making symbols that ultimately create what we recognize as words, phrases, and other components of a writing system. Although the tools of writing have changed over time, to inscribe entails physical activity (or a substitute that creates an inscription, such as in the case of you verbally dictating your creative writing).

While all that you do as a creative writer includes things beyond that physical inscribing, ultimately you cannot be a creative writer without those actions of inscribing. It is nevertheless relatively unremarkable to meet an aspirant creative writer who has not taken action, who is perpetually *going to* write a novel, or a poem, or a short story, a children's book, a film script, a song. You might wonder if you would come across the same magnitude of unfulfilled human ambition if you were an automotive engineer, a bus driver, a chemistry professor, or a nurse. 'Hey, now there's a coincidence, I'm going to design and build a fuel efficient sports car too!' 'Next week I'm absolutely going to start to drive a bus.' 'I've always wanted to do some catalytic hydrogenation.' 'Actually, I also spend a lot of my time planning to facilitate healing.'

Human aspirations are of course many and varied, sometimes they are even miraculous. Therefore, it is not the aspiration to be a creative writer that is in itself remarkable. Rather, it is what is behind the aspiration and the associative desires it represents. Action has to triumph over inaction to see that aspiration and those desires met. In some types of creative writing actions come about because of industry need, an imperative beyond your writing self. For example, Warren Leight, a television writer whose credits include scripts for *Law & Order: Special Victims Unit*, the crime drama set in New York City and now beyond its twentieth TV season, comments:

> I have writer's block when there's no deadline. I have as much block as I can afford within the structure of having to shoot it on Monday (laugh). You really can't have writer's block when you're shooting it on Monday and it's Friday night. You just keep writing until it's finished. (Kallas, 2014: 45)

While a detailed study of unfulfilled but aspirant creative writers would almost certainly reveal to us more detail, simply think here of the combination of factors the aspiration to be a creative writer presents.

Firstly, while there are many terms and expressions we associate with the creative it is significant that 'creative writing' uses the word 'creative' so directly. Such a direct definitional use clearly highlights, differentiates (that is, creative writing from other forms of writing), declares, addresses, and identifies. To choose to express a desire to write creatively suggests your intention to undertake certain kinds of actions with certain intended results. Had you expressed a desire to do some report writing or essay writing or journalistic writing the explicit and implicit associations would not be the same as those expressed by the term 'creative writing'. For example, the difference could be in relation to accuracy or to straightforwardness. You have differentiated your plans, and you have directly declared them. You have also addressed questions, however generally, of expectation – yours and those of your potential readership/audience. Were you therefore then to produce an essay or a report it could be that you, or anyone else who encountered it, would wonder why it did not show traits associated with a genre identified as creative writing. Significantly, you have also identified yourself as a (potential) creative writer.

The description 'creative writer' relates to an individual as well as cultural type, and a creative writer's identity goes beyond the actual practices of creative writing and carries with it the weight of historical and contemporary archetypes. How many people do not take action to be creative writers because they feel they do not fit the mold of what a creative writer is, or how a creative writer generally behaves? Perhaps nobody! On the other hand, consider your conception of a creative writer and what you believe about a creative writer's daily life. Imagine a poet and imagine a screenwriter and honestly answer if you believe there is a difference – not simply between what they write but between who they are. Of course, this all presses toward not archetype but stereotype. Nevertheless, the key point is undiminished. We believe certain things about creative writing, we declare certain things when we use the definition 'creative writing', and we suggest a certain identity when we describe others or ourselves as 'a creative writer', sometimes a specific kind of creative writer. These definitions highlight, differentiate, declare, address, and identify. Your actions come about when you are attuned to the definitions, enlivened by them, perhaps even feeling personally and culturally empowered by them. Inaction comes about when you are not attuned to the definitions, unfamiliar with or unsure about navigating the compositional practices associated with a chosen genre of creative writing, perhaps even uncomfortable or unsure of the personal propensities suggested by the definitions. Inaction in these senses is the result of a combination of psychological and cultural influences, the current state of your technical ability and localized issues raised by your choice of genre, your generic intentions not ultimately matched by your familiarity, your curiosity, and your determination that supports your interest in a subject or theme.

Secondly, inaction can outweigh action when the gaps between what you think and sense, and understand from your experience, and what you creatively envision and inventively form are not bridged. We see evidence of this in the initial forays into creative writing by avant-gardist

Alan Burns, who published eight novels, two books of non-fiction, and a play in a writing career spanning the second half of the twentieth century, writing in ways often indeed described as 'experimental'. He comments:

> I began writing short prose pieces in a rather pressured, affected style, trying to say something significant in every sentence. One piece was about digging a hole in the ground; one described a man rowing a boat. I started with something seen, then isolated and intensified it … I realized I could hang around for ever waiting for things to happen that would trigger off precious paragraphs. (Gordon, 1975: 63)

The aspiration to be a creative writer involves a combination of your imagination and your intellect; and your actions involve both of these, in a combination that is fluid and integrated. We can think of this as a network in which synapses are located. Synapses are intersections permitting sparks of transmission, triggers at junctures, transmitted there between cognition and vision, your thoughts and your feelings. These synaptic points provide for the combination of envisioning and critical assessment that we know to be involved in creative writing. Simply, because writing is a tool that involves the use of language in cogently inscribed ways so that signs and symbols it uses are widely recognizable, and *creative* writing involves the imaginative use of both language and that tool that is writing, then both creativity and intellect are at work. The intellect is associated with the rational and logical, whereas creativity involves feeling and memory, divergent as well as convergent thinking, uniqueness and originality, as well as the conventional and paradigmatic.

If the synaptic transmissions do not happen, the imaginative and the intellectual are not communicating across a juncture; if creative and or critical knowledge does not allow the tool that is writing to best be employed, then it is natural that as creative writers we produce inaction rather than action. We see discussion of this phenomenon in the history of instructional works about creative writing when we read references to 'writer's block', or to moments when a creative writer appears unable to see issues with a draft of a work, or to how reading aloud can sometimes better show strengths and weaknesses in a draft. All these references are in fact substitutes for analyzing how your inaction is the product of a lack of empowering junctures, a failure to trigger synapses that make it possible for you to be a creative writer.

Thirdly, inaction can occur when you are less confident or less familiar with a genre, a type, a form, a style, a tone, a technique. The synapses that allow for communication between the imaginative and the intellectual are connected with your ideas, thoughts, feelings, observations, senses. It is in these that connectivity is generated because you seek to portray events and actions, responses and reflections that are related to your subjects and themes. But familiarity and confidence are more likely associated not with subject or theme, not with your content, but with compositional technique and your written language use. In this way, familiarity and confidence relate to the tool you have chosen – that tool is writing, and a specific kind of writing – and how you proceed in using that tool. The synaptic interchange between your imagination and your intellect when writing creatively makes your choice of tool complex. However, it is nevertheless useful to consider the basics, and therefore to imagine any task you plan to undertake and how much your familiarity with and confidence in the tools you will use influences and supports your actions. Imagine trying to build a cabin without confidence in using a saw and a hammer; or trying to construct a computer program without any familiarity with computer code.

Writing is a tool and creative writing is a specific kind of tool. If you are unsure how to use the tool, how aspects of it will act when you have them in use, then it is more likely you'll pause, or ultimately baulk at a creative writing task. It is also more likely you will become frustrated with the process, unhappy with your progress or that you will feel unable to resolve technical issues that arise.

Tools are used to carry out functions, and our human ability to invent and employ tools that are ever more sophisticated is one of the reasons for our long-term success as a species. In this vein, Pulitzer Prize-winning novelist Annie Dillard begins her book *The Writing Life* by remarking that 'when you write, you lay out a line of words. The line of words is a miner's pick, a woodcarver's gouge, a surgeon's probe' (Dillard, 1989: 3). Tools, in other words. Tools have a metaphoric presence as well as a physical one, because they are also figuratively associated with construction, with our evolution, and with our physical engagement with the world. As a creative writer your familiarity and confidence in compositional techniques and written language is therefore informed by metaphoric association as well as literal understanding. The psychological depth of this is considerable, given that the emotional and transcendental aspects of creativity are combined here with your intellectual engagement. Is it any wonder so many of what we have called 'how-to' books about creative writing seek not only to offer you technical advice but also to bolster your self-confidence? What the authors of these books have detected is the affective-analytical synapses needed to take action as a creative writer, and what they have recognized is that these synapses do not always happen. What they have missed is that to resolve this you cannot only improve technical competency and/or improve your self-esteem; you need to address the association between your rational thoughts, your feelings, and your memories, to work on synaptic communication between the logical conventions of writing and the imaginative originality of your personal world.

Finally, creative writing can best be considered an event in which actions takes place. Events occur in space and time. Events have degrees of significance. An event can incorporate constant activity, a pattern of activities, or periods of action and inaction. Considering creative writing as an event, you can focus on causes and effects, so that each aspect of your approach to your creative writing has an individual and integrated context. The ancient meaning of event incorporates the notion of a result, and in this way, thinking of creative writing as an event also emphasizes that you are aiming to achieve something. In other words, that you have an intention. There is also a particularity about an event, so that events have a character, a condition that can be analyzed in terms of such things as the habitat of the event and the actions that take place within the event. Events also have a shape. In their entirety, this involves a beginning, a middle, and an end. We can talk of actions that are 'pre-event', 'part of the event', and 'post-event' and, in creative writing terms, come to a better understanding of your compositional patterns.

The Event of Creative Writing

With creative writing being an event, it can be understood in terms of the nature of events. Events have an origin as well as a cause – what is most often referred to as an 'antecedent', suggesting not only that something came before but that it had significance for you, and that it created the conditions where a desire to write became the actions of creative writing. Because creative writing is a specific kind of writing, its antecedents involve writing choices that, to be successful, are conscious writing choices. There is nothing extraordinary about that, in that writing generally is a system; and therefore, as a system, it involves your conscious effort. However, because creative writing is powered by creative interpretations and artistic responses, the choices available to you are greater, both within the paradigms of particular creative writing genre and sometimes in creatively spurring you to challenge those paradigms.

The impetus for your creative writing might be an observation, a memory, a feeling, or a combination of any number of these and other things. In fact, what causes the event of your creative writing is as individual as each creative writer. Diarist, essayist, and fiction writer Anaïs Nin once wrote:

> We write to taste life twice, in the moment, and in retrospection … We write to be able to transcend our life, to reach beyond it. We write to teach ourselves to speak to others, to record our journey into the labyrinth. (Holt, 2006: 54)

The antecedents of your creative writing might be very clear to you, or their character, extent, and influence might in some way be hidden, part of a network of inspirations, motivations, prompts. Of course, you will have intentions for your creative writing, and your individual intentions can be categorized in ways that reflect goals that other creative writers will often share; such as the widespread goal of expressing an emotion in a satisfying way, or the common goal of entertaining a perceived audience, or the goal of revealing a truth or truths, or the goal of earning an income from your creative activities, or the simple goal of recording an event.

The event of creative writing contains the actions you undertake, as well as those things that occur that are not initiated, sustained, or controlled by you – because serendipity and fortuitousness certainly occur too. Your pattern of creative composition can begin any time, long before you initiate the physical actions of creative writing or immediately before those actions. One event of creative writing might lead to or intersect with others, with each at different composition stages. You might see the event of creative writing as a discrete part of your day or night, or an integrated part. For you, the event of creative writing might involve a distinct set of circumstances of time and place, of psychological and physiological conditions, so that your mental and physical state is most conducive to what you are attempting to accomplish. South African writer and political activist Nadine Gordimer talks about the pattern of mental and physical event of creative writing when she says:

> I think it's a habit. It's kind of a discipline, so that I do work regularly, and when I don't seem to be working, then probably I still am, too. You tend to measure yourself – all writers do – by what you actually have put down on paper, how many words. But I don't think that's when the work's

really done. It's done at other times. It's happening sometimes at the back of ordinary, everyday living, while you're talking to someone, or while you're going about some daily chore you have to do – meeting the world in some way. Then you're carrying on your work behind it. I think the two run concurrently. (Bazin and Seymour, 1990: 18)

If for a moment the complexity of the event at all seems overstated, consider how complex the interaction between the imaginative and intellectual is in creative writing, and how everyday the tool you are using. Our written language, its many marks and symbols, is designed for as wide as possible sense and transfer, for complementing our spoken language, and for creating more enduring records within a language culture or group. As a creative writer, you take that writing system and, while most often maintaining the desire for making sense and for transferring your meaning, empower that system to be more inventive, more exploratory, more original. The event that is creative writing is in this way multifaceted. This is partially why we are so fascinated by creative writers' quirks, superstitions, and stories of how particular works were created. Certainly also because the fame of a completed work draws our attention to the writer behind it. But there, behind it, we find elements of the event of creative writing that emphasizes the individuality of the practice.

Thinking of creative writing as your individually defined event, you can gain greater knowledge of its main elements:

Structure – Where the event of your creative writing begins, what constitutes the bulk of it, the larger part, and how the event of your creative writing ends. Whether different projects – and the event of creative writing associated with them or incorporating them – intersect, overlap, or overlay each other, in what ways and to what effect. For example, does your creative writing work best when individual projects are composed discretely or is there creative and/or critical energy generated in the connections between your multiple projects?

Duration – How long does creative writing take? You can read a deal of critical thought that attaches significance to duration in creative writing. Usually this is divided between those assessments that view overall effort as defining the quality of a finished work, and those that attach duration to a particular creative writing genre. None of this is not standardized, but the common approach is to associate longer lengths of composition time with the writing of novels, perhaps screenplays, epic poems rather than shorter poetic forms like haiku or sonnets. Thinking of duration from a creative writing practice point of view is not necessarily going to produce the same approach or assessment.

From a creative writer's point of view, the duration of a particular event of creative writing is determined by the number of compositional labors, the impact of wider personal circumstances, perhaps the familiarity with a particular topic or theme, experience also with the chosen genre. This list here is likewise individualized rather than standardized, and the reasoning is distinctive to creative writing rather than a post-event assessment of the quality of the finished product or the place of that genre in a canon of cultural artifacts. Approaching duration in creative writing this way better explains how projects happen, and how duration is defined by you and assessed by you to inform your compositional strategies. In a September 2016 article in *Business Insider*, focusing on readers waiting for the next book by *A Game of Thrones* (1996) writer George R.R. Martin, Jacob Shamsian noted that Martin 'writes at a rate of less than three pages per day'. An infographic included in the same article shows wide variations in writing duration, with a work such as Robert Louis Stevenson's *The Strange Case of Dr Jekyll and Mr Hyde* up toward one end of the spectrum, taking six days to complete, and J.D. Salinger's *Catcher in the Rye* up toward the other end, taking ten years (Shamsian, 2016).

Span – Whether episodes in your creative writing are inaugural, disruptive, and uncommon, the kind of episodes that happen singularly, perhaps for the first time, and usually not for long. For example, you visit somewhere for the first time during the composition of a work, or you try a new writing technique or you aim to address a theme you have not addressed previously. Episodes as you write can also be recurring, or cyclic. In that regard, your compositional approach might have a relatively set pattern from first draft to completed draft. Finally, some episodes in the event of your creative writing might not be episodic at all; but rather, are part of a continuum of action. In this sense, your creative writing will include aspects of your daily life, relationships, and work patterns that are sustained over considerable time. Understanding the interaction between the disruptive, the recurring, and the sustained helps you to assess the role and impact of each of these aspects on your creative writing.

Order – Your creative writing will be an event with an order. That is not to say that order remains the same for every writing experience, or that the order is necessarily fixed regardless of external influences and fortuitous circumstances. Simply, by and large creative writers attempt to order the event of creative writing, not least because the interaction between the imagination and intellect is fluid and creatively empowered while writing is a definite, shared system of communication and expression. Ordering assists you in bringing together the creative and the critical to reach your intended goals.

Enactment – Because it communicates between the creative writer and a reader or audience, the event of creative writing involves performance, or what you can think of as the public and enduring presentation of what would otherwise be your private thoughts, feelings, and responses to the world. Thinking about the event of creative writing as a performance, taking things from the internal world to the external, orchestrating these things to appeal to someone other than ourselves, adopting voices, tones, personas (narrators, characters) to contribute to the performance, ensures an event can be enacted. A poet and memoirist who was also a singer, Maya Angelou, invokes this idea of performance when she says:

> I write for the Black voice and any ear which can hear it. As a composer writes for musical instruments and a choreographer creates for the body, I search for sound, tempos, and rhythms to ride through the vocal cord over the tongue, and out of the lips of Black people. (Evans, 1985: 3–4)

Participation – Is it only you who participates in your event of creative writing? Some creative writers work with others throughout the process. Some engage family, friends, or colleagues as key members of the compositional 'team' at certain points, reading drafts, discussing themes or subjects, even drawing on family or community members as models for attitudes, appearances, associations in an otherwise fictional work. In 1934 F. Scott Fitzgerald wrote to literary critic Christian Gauss, a frequent Fitzgerald correspondent, that 'there comes a time when a writer writes for certain people and where the opinion of the others is of little less than no importance at all' (Phillips, 1988: 82). Clearly Fitzgerald declaring his desire to be independent of much external critical opinion!

How actively you participate in your event of creative writing also varies over time and space and in terms of particular actions. You might spend a great deal of time preparing to draft a work and very little time redrafting it. Alternatively, you might be a creative writer who begins drafting almost immediately and then reworks that first draft many times. Compositional strategies recall technical preferences – which relate to your personal sense of how to shape an idea, make an imaginative leap, tell a story, recall and create an image. There are psychological as well as aesthetic reasons why you choose to participate more in one element of the event of creative writing than in another. There is no right or wrong weighing up of your participation; although, frequently, the suggestion that creative writing involves hard work means that the image of the writerly craftsperson meticulously and sometimes laboriously working on each component of their process is not uncommon. Such an idea is not untrue; it is simply that it is not universally or consistently accurate, and both artistic and communicative practices are far more individualized than this.

Because creative writing is an event that takes place in time and space, has a pattern of activities, always including some physical action or analogues for physical action, and has a shape determined by its duration and the order of activities, we can examine our creative writing actions according to whether they are *pre-event, during the event*, or *post-event*.

Pre-creative writing can include those actions that occur chronologically around your creative writing antecedents. In other words, while they are not the origin or cause of your creative writing, they are the reason for you being in a particular place, or the influences that cause you to consider a certain story or image or character, or come to investigate an event, or to seek out more about a topic, or to read something that influences your thinking or your emotions, or to engage with a historical fact, or to be open to the actions of creative writing that follow. Simply, pre-creative writing is that which occurs before the event of creative writing but might in some way have a connection to it, providing a hinterland to the writing itself and placing your event of creative writing in context, so that the compositional aspects of your creative writing might be understood, from the point of their initiation to the point of their conclusion.

The event of creative writing itself can be said to begin at the point at which your actions are directly related to a writing project, and to end when you release that work in some way from your grasp. This release might be when you feel you have completed as much work on a piece of creative writing as you can bear to complete, or when you feel the work is as well-done as it is likely to become, or when you are called upon to deliver something for publication or performance, or when your projected reader/audience is at hand and you have to finish in order to present your work to them. The event of your creative writing here is presented as if it is one event; but, of course, a number of projects might overlap or overlay each other, influencing or informing each other. During the event of creative writing, your actions incorporate imaginative engagement as well as intellectual assessments. You behave in a more or less identifiable way, some actions borne out of practices you might have long undertaken, some part of a cycle of compositional activity, one action being brought about by another, and others specific to a project in a way that disrupts your normal practice, or introduces new modes of composing, or brings to the fore ideas or feelings or investigations that you have not previously encountered or undertaken.

Post-creative writing is those things, those actions, and often also those reactions that occur after an event of creative writing concludes. Post-creative writing, from your creative writer's point of view, can include your own assessment of your otherwise completed work, sometimes putting it back into the role of being 'incomplete', conceptually, even though you don't return to it but simply envisage you might have done some things different. Post-creative writing is also the point at which you might discover aspects of your practice – at least as evidenced by the final work and the drafts and supporting materials that lead up to that final work – that you hadn't noticed during the practice, or feel you had undertaken differently in your previous creative writing, or you recognize as the result of influences that were not before known to you. Post-creative writing is also where you might respond, openly and immediately or otherwise, to the reactions of others to your work. It is here, of course, where most reaction from others occurs, so it is here where you most likely will consider critical opinion, critique those critiques by others, consider if what others are seeing corresponds with your own thoughts. In some cases, post-creative writing can be the beginning of your next project, your next creative writing event, perhaps because your next creative writing is initiated by your realization that there is more to say or explore on a subject or a feeling or a response to the world; perhaps because other subjects, feelings, or responses emerge during writing that the current project isn't appropriate to house. For the creative writer – who by definition must continue to write creatively or no longer be a creative writer – post-creative writing is not so much a lull in the storm as a recognition that a new event of creative writing is about to start. Whatever might or might not have been learnt from those creative writing events that came before will color future writerly actions.

Actions and Acts

We can differentiate here between actions and acts. Your actions of creative writing are individual and they are specific. That is, there are things you *do*, and each of these actions has an individual character, purpose, and projected result. While individual, each of your actions is undertaken in the context of your other actions, and each in some way reflects your thoughts, your feelings, and the strengths of your technical abilities in creative writing.

Actions of creative writing are many, and some are very well known. These include those associated with your use of the basics of written language, your creation of recognizable grammatical units (the forming of phrases, clauses, and sentences, for example), to the releasing of final works of creative writing in particular formats that are recognizable by those who work in such industries as publishing or the media. Other actions of creative writing are more mysterious, bearing the distinctive characteristics of the imaginative, the visionary, what can even be described as transcendental. These actions, that draw on or empower the imagination and that involve taking the relatively day-to-day tool of a shared written language and making it a creative tool, are threaded throughout the event of creative writing and form the basis of how creative writing is a distinct form of writing.

Your imaginative action can include such things as making metaphoric connections in thinking and acting on questions of subject or theme or in structuring a work. Metaphor shifts the plane of reference, while maintaining an association with literal meaning. By doing this, it deepens the examination and understanding of things or phenomena. So a poem seeking to expose a political injustice explores aspects of justice in the natural world, or a novel is structured according to the physical shape and movements through a suburban street. Metaphoric composition can be thought of as imaginative action. Imaginative action can also include speculative leaps, those 'What if?' questions you might ask that might not be supported by evidence, but by being asked in creative writing open up avenues of thought or quicken feeling. Creating new associations between content or traversing disparate themes can likewise be the result of imaginative action.

In these ways, the actions of creative writing include that brought about by creativity and that brought about by intellectual engagement. Creative writing is in effect an entwinement of action and thought and feeling. Further still, it is the product of physical action that emphasizes dexterity, so much so that creative writing has often been described not only as an 'art' but also as a 'craft', to emphasize a creative writer's manual skills. This notion situates whatever thought and feeling you have at work literally in your hands, as a creative writer; and, although not all creative writing requires the use of your hands, and much has evolved in the equipment we use to undertake creative writing, that idea of creative writing being a craft emphasizes physical action.

Actions are defined as your individual, specific occurrences. Acts are defined as an accumulation of your actions around a sequence or evolution of the work. Just like in a stage play, an opera, or a film, an act is associated with movements in the action or development of characters or patterns of evolution in emotions or ideas or steps toward resolutions. Whereas considering creative writing an event allows us to focus on the various episodes in an event of writing, and all the elements these episodes include, identifying acts allows us to determine how sets of actions relate to each other, and in what ways the content of your creative writing relates to the labor of producing it. In other words, an act of creative writing can refer both to the internal aspects of the piece you are creating *and* to sets of compositional actions you are undertaking to move the piece forward to a conclusion.

There is good reason for thinking of creative writing in this actions-within-acts way. In essence, the actions of drafting, revising, and editing have both a forward movement and a sideways movement. You are moving forward with the sense of your intention to complete a work, while at the same time approaching it holistically, sometimes cantilevering so as to further support later events or references in the work. As you draft, revise, and edit, your compositional actions are both seeking to reach an endpoint and seeking to ensure what comes before sustains the movement toward that conclusion. It might be that you have planned this out meticulously and the first compositional act of your creative writing is that very aspect of planning. It might be that you don't plan at all, but that your first act in your creative writing contains a foray into defining the sense of the work through drafting exploration. In the latter case you're learning the work as you create it. In the former sense you're endeavoring to learn it before you create it. It might be that you can determine the acts of your creative writing by defining those actions you regard as drafting – where things are relatively fluid, and much is flux and evolving – and those you regard as components of revising – where what you have written is subject to reconsideration and recasting – and those actions you include in the act of editing – where the aim is to bring a work to a finish, reaffirm, and add any final strengthening to some or all of its elements.

Compositional acts suggest a sequence of actions but actions can also be repeated. Often this is a case of compositional resonance, you bringing to bear the same writing techniques for a different part of the composition. For instance, you look to create expositional background at particular points in the work or employ figurative language. You might introduce rising action in a plot in line with certain genre conventions. Your writing of a poem could associate formal structure with structured methods and repeat the structural characteristics in tandem with your methods of composition throughout.

Because at some point you must take action in order to be a creative writer, creative writing is, ultimately, your actions. Novelist Philip Roth suggests that such action might not appear immediately productive, commenting: 'I often have to write a hundred pages or more before there's a paragraph that's alive ... I look for the liveliness to set the tone' (Plimpton, 1986: 271).

To understand your actions further, to develop these further, to undertake these actions with more knowledge and more application to your intentions, you can investigate the structure of the event that is your creative writing. When does it begin, what constitutes the bulk of it, and how does the event of such writing end? From your point of view, how long does creative writing take? Which episodes in this event are inaugural, disruptive, and uncommon, which are recurring, which part something sustained over considerable time? What is the pattern of this relationship? What order are these episodes in your event of creative writing? What elements of enactment or performance occur, that take your personal thoughts and feelings and make them public? Who participates in your writing – you alone or you and others? Finally, what are your actions, that array of individual things you do, and how are these actions brought into a series of acts, containing actions that are unique to one act and actions that are resonant, occurring again and again throughout the event of your creative writing?

Exploring Action

- Because creative writing is an event it is made of actions and those actions elicit reactions. The fluidity of the movement between the creative and the intellectual means that some of those reactions will be imaginative and some analytical.
- Any event occurs in time and in space. Creative writing is no different: it occurs according to a length of time, in some kind of sequence of actions, and at some place. This simple observation allows us to explore the context of any compositional moment and consider why we are doing what we are doing.
- Being a specific kind of writing, it is useful to consider the acts in your creative writing in terms of what techniques are being employed and why in any one act of creative writing, given that some will be commonplace actions within the writing system and transcendent actions.
- Inaction has origins and reasons, and understanding these helps us address them. If you do not at some point take action, you will not at some point be a creative writer. No question.

3

Emotion

Feeling, Belief, Motivation

In formal analysis, anecdotes are often frowned upon for lacking critical depth. And yet, an anecdote is also thought to reveal experiences and to connect individuals personally in ways that structured, formal analysis mostly does not. With that in mind, and as seems appropriate in a chapter entitled 'Emotion', here then is an anecdote.

Around twenty years ago a well-known TV books program asked some writers of literary fiction to attempt to write a Mills & Boon novel. As many will know, Mills & Boon is a publisher of romance novels. Founded in 1908, with its headquarters in the United Kingdom, the company publishes hundreds of these romance titles every year, their considerable popularity as books and more recently as e-books belying the fact that much critical opinion has dismissed these novels not only as formulaic but also as portraying women and sexuality in ways that range from gross stereotyping to the active encouragement of fantasies involving rape. Needless to say, the strength of these responses between a readership that has made these some of the most popular works of creative writing in the world and critics, some of whom offer nothing less than condemnation, makes for an interesting study. What was of particular interest to the TV books program, however, was the way in which these works were written, who was able to write them well (given that 'writing a Mills & Boon novel well' meant something distinct and relatively unambiguous), and how much the writing of them could be replicated. After all, if the works were in fact formulaic and if they were presenting simplistic interpretations of relationship themes and subjects, surely any reasonably competent creative writer could write one?

The TV program therefore sent away four writers, all of whom had credentials as writers of published novels determined to have strong literary merit. Because Mills & Boon releases guidelines to assist its aspiring authors, and includes additional advice for those targeting its individual series, such as Medical Romance, Vintage, and Blaze (where sexual topics are more prominent), the available support for these potential new Mills & Boon creative writers was considerable. A few weeks passed, then the TV program had the four writers back on set to talk about their experiences. The outcomes were universally less than wonderful, although they varied a little.

Intention is a key component of creative writing. Action is another. Without an understanding of what you intend and why you intend it, and without actually acting upon it, and ultimately producing some physical response, quite simply by *doing it*, creative writing does not happen. However, creative writing is also dependent on your emotional engagement – in some form, and because the imagination and human creativity transcend logic and reason, and in doing so engage parts of the brain that logic does not. With this in mind, it is perhaps no surprise that the creative writers who had been offered the task of writing a Mills & Boon novel found it difficult when they couldn't emotionally engage with the task.

Of the four writers who attempted to write this particular version of a romance novel, all four reported varying degrees of failure. For three of them, their failure was all but complete. Each said they had not managed to progress anything worth reporting, in spite of a number of attempts and regardless of their identifiable strong creative writing skills evidenced in their previous personal projects. Each of these three reported difficulty making the guidelines work for them, though they noted that these guidelines were clear enough, and at least one reported being unable 'to take this seriously'. The fourth writer reported something a little different. They had progressed something, and said they were even thinking of trying to complete it. They were unsure if it was what was required, or even if what they had written matched the requirements, but they thought they would at least finish the work and see what others thought of it. Studied bemusement might be the best way to describe their response to the experiment. They believed they had somehow managed to channel what they felt was their more natural writing inclinations and to match the Mills & Boon guidelines. They were unsure of the value of having done that, and not sure they would or should do it again.

What was clear, and is clear more broadly from this story, is that these creative writers didn't believe in Mills & Boon novels, that they had no emotional investment in writing a work of that kind, and that their motivation for attempting this experiment was artificial and unsatisfying. While they might well have had considerable creative writing skills, the majority couldn't bridge the credibility gap created by their lack of feeling for the effort, and the only writer who could make progress questioned their belief in the results and their motivation to continue.

Feeling, belief, and motivation are integral to creative writing because creative writing is a form of writing that at its core deals in both the tangible and the intangible. Tangible, in that such creative writing techniques and schema such as plot, character, setting, exposition have a tangible existence; intangible, in that creative writing explores your perceptions and senses, as well as your ideas. In that respect, creative writing is informed by your emotions. Emotions are conscious and manifest themselves in both psychological and physical ways.

Feeling – Feelings and emotions are sometimes treated as interchangeable. However, emotion involves mental processing that brings about conscious assessments and then results in a reaction. Your feelings are not reasoned in that way, but they are nevertheless responses. Feeling tends to be highly individualized, whereas emotions can be described in more universal and humanly instinctual ways, even if they are given your individual expression and embodiment. Your feelings are how you describe and respond to your emotions, and in that sense these descriptions are influenced by your personality and by your experiences. What is described by one person as fear might be described by another person as apprehension, even though the sense data being received is the same. This is more than simply labeling, because these descriptions of feeling shape our engagement with the world around us, and determine how we respond to the sensory experiences we have and the processing of information we receive.

Creative writing draws on both the processing of the intellect, and in this way is associated with emotion, as well as the creativity and intangible responses of the imagination, and in this way is associated with feeling. Novelist, poet, and translator Vladimir Nabokov recalls something of this when he speaks about the writer's exchange with the reader:

> It seems to me that a good formula to test the quality of a novel is, in the long run, a merging of the precision of poetry and the intuition of science. In order to bask in that magic a wise reader reads the book of genius not with his heart, not so much with his brain, but with his spine. (Nabokov, 1980: 6)

In order to write, given that writing involves reasoned action, you need to control feeling, as much as understand your emotions. Your feelings are inspired by situations and informed by your memories. This is one of the reasons why creative writing, engaging feeling, is not always as easy to undertake as it is at other times. It is not only a case of technical competency or ability it is also a case of engaging and controlling feeling. To take the Mills & Boon experiment as an example: the creative writers in the experiment both responded according to emotions, where they processed the task and the projected results and largely rejected these, and they had feelings about the effort, based on what is often colloquially called 'gut reaction'. They also lacked belief.

Belief – Creative writing relies on belief on several levels. Firstly, much of creative writing involves suspending disbelief in order to explore situations, scenarios, fictional versions of people and places, with the aim of articulating, revealing, examining and manifesting ideas, events and mental states. Without belief, and therefore a shared agreement between writer and audience in having suspended it, this exercise would have little veracity. Secondly, there is your basic belief in the practice and outcomes of creative writing itself. Because undertaking such writing is a conscious choice, and 'accidental' creative writing tends not to be fit for purpose, the belief that it has a purpose, and that it is worthwhile, informs that conscious choice. Thirdly, there is the belief in specific elements of creative writing – examples include belief in the genre you choose and how that relates to your intentions; belief in the ways in which such writing moves between the imaginative and the intellect; your belief in the methods by which finished works of creative writing reach their readers/audience. Such belief here might also be your confidence in particular creative writing techniques and processes in relation to your trust in their influence and impact. Finally, there is the demonstrated situation where you need to believe in the results, to believe not only in the practices of an event of creative writing but also in the intended outcome of it. Such a belief is key to sustaining yourself as a creative writer in situations where investigations of content or consideration of theme or themes or development of new or difficult writing techniques or quite simply the labor involved asks for your personal continued motivation – your sustained action.

Motivation – Just because you believe in something and have positive feelings for it does not mean you're actually going to do anything about it. The chances of undertaking some creative writing are of course increased by your positive feelings for creative writing; but your actions involve your motivation, which is broadly defined as an influence or compulsion. Satirist, biographer, journalist and noted literary stylist Evelyn Waugh commented in *Nash's Pall Mall Magazine* in March 1937, ironically given his talents and given also that five months later the magazine ceased publication, having been published in some form since 1893:

> I was driven into writing because it was the only way a lazy and ill-educated man could make a decent living. I am not complaining about the wages. They always seemed to me disproportionately high. What I mind so much is the work. (Holt, 2006: 66)

Your motivation to be a creative writer combines a number of influences, from the biological to the cultural. These motivations are both intrinsic and extrinsic. For you, these could begin with your most basic needs – for instance, your desire to write as part of a survival strategy in which your creative writing produces an income. In that case, your writing is clearly associated with your basic human needs – in itself, or through your connected activities such as teaching creative writing or a cognate field. Such survival needs are not necessarily the strongest motivation for the majority of those undertaking some creative writing because the majority of creative writers do not rely directly on their creative writing for their primary employment. Nevertheless, the common notion of such writing being something that must be worked at to be successful also carries this same work ethic into ideals of motivation. So, while your motivation might not relate to a direct survival strategy, to the providing of your basic needs, the societal perception of creative writing as involving considerable, time-consuming, personally invested labor informs a sense in which the practice takes on a similar significance.

Incentivizing can come about, of course, from rewards that are not financial, not so directly related to basic survival needs. The rewards from creative writing can be intensely personal, and can include such motivating causes as the reliving of a valued memory, the productive or playful imagining of an alternative scenario and the belief in creating a bond with others through sharing experiences, ideas and emotions. Creative writing is often culturally well respected as a practice, and so carries with it kudos that is satisfying as well as motivating. Additionally, creative writing is a practice that projects into the future – most obviously, the future when the writing you are undertaking is complete and you have a finished work in front of you. In that way, it comes with expectations and a sense of future accomplishment, which is bolstered by the positive cultural status of creativity and of creative writing specifically, and is buoyed by a sense in which the ability to use written language well enough to be a creative writer is a valuable personal and societal capability.

Creative writing involves the animation of your feelings, your thoughts and your creativity. That animation provides stimulation; and the focus on newness, the originality associated with creativity, brings with it a sense of renewal. Your motivation is activated and enlivened by these things; and because written language is not always used to enliven this way, to originate, the specific conditions of creative writing make the animation associated with it even more evocative. Thinking this way, your actions of creative writing can be said to incite, to revive and to awaken. It is a common belief that when we are not enlivened by our own creative writing our readers or audience will not be either. This belief is one heard in the teaching of creative writing. The truth of this is located in the psychology and physiology of motivation, whereby we humans seek heightened experiences that stimulate us mentally and physically. The popularity of sports, and a variety of leisure pursuits, likewise reminds us of this element of human behavior. However, creative writing carries the additional and distinctive element of intellectual engagement and communicative ability. Its status as art suggests both a personal importance and a desire to share experiences, ideas, observations, and discoveries with others.

Emotion, Emotional, Emotive

You come across a poem published online. It is lacking much in the way of interesting content or compelling themes, uses an overabundance of descriptive words, adjectives that are seemingly attempting to qualify but do not quite evoke or clarify or explain anything much at all. In what appears to be the final published draft, the poem is unsuccessful. Although you sense there was something moving and poignant that the writer was trying to portray, the piece fails to touch you, and equally fails to convey any substantive content or theme.

As it turns out, a short time later you meet the poet responsible for the poem. Perhaps tentatively, being embarrassed, you mention you happened to be online and you read a poem they had written, and you mention it by name. At that point, the poet tells you that the writing of that poem was the highpoint of their writing life to date, that they hope you enjoyed it, and that the poem says everything they wanted to say in a way they wanted to say it.

What is happening here?

It is of course somewhat stereotyping to tell a story of an overwrought poem and an affected poet. Of all the creative writing types it is poetry that is most often portrayed as being subject to the gushy or schmaltzy. In reality, any type of writing might be the focus of this story. Depending on the writer's personal intention, the poem might, at least in terms of meeting that writer's intentions, be considered either unsuccessful or successful. Clearly, the writer in this instance considers the poem has been successful – for them. What the story suggests, however, is that the emotional engagement for the writer is not matched by successful communication with a reader – in this case, you.

While in this example it is possible to recognize the validity of both the literary analysis point of view (the negative response based on the final text) and the creative writer's point of view (the positive response by the creative writer based on meeting their intention), the public nature of the work (the poet has published it online) suggests it is entirely valid to assess the success of the work based on whether it communicates successfully with its reader. That judgment is complex, and includes elements of whether it appeals to a reader's senses, whether it can be defined by them as 'beautiful', whether in attempting to communicate something through creative writing its purpose is achieved. Each of these judgments can be shared ones – readers agreeing widely on a response – or individual ones – the poem appealing to one reader but not to another. This strays from the topic of emotion here more into questions of judgment. Immanuel Kant's classic text on the subject, *Critique of Judgement* (1952, first published 1790), provides a productive starting point for further exploration of critiques of judgment related to such concepts as purposefulness and reflection. But here the focus is on emotion and your emotional engagement as a creative writer, and the example of the online poem highlights a salient point. That is, when intended as communication with others, creative writing is not merely the outpouring of feeling empowered by your emotions. Rather, creative writing involves you structuring written language, and because this written language is reliant on collective communication, because if you seek to exchange your thoughts, feelings, observations and ideas that written language has to transfer to individual groups and indeed individual people, creative writing cannot mainly be an outpouring of feeling. This means that in order to reach audiences for your works of creative writing you have to understand and be able to access the emotions behind your feelings, comprehend something of how others might respond to such emotional contexts, and then act successfully upon your understanding using your technical skills and knowledge and in relation to particular creative writing forms and genre.

The imagination, which is core to creative writing's methods and its written distinctiveness, both assists and potentially undermines your efforts to engage with and employ emotion. This is because the imagination must so strongly initiate and engage feeling. It does so because in order to produce mental images of things and activities that are not immediately accessible there is a need for an intensity of mental activity beyond the ordinary. Your creative writing is dependent on such an intensity of feeling and an engagement with your emotions, while at the same time you need to channel this feeling and engagement in a mode of expression and communication that relies on organizational techniques and expressive modes that are not about an emotional outpouring.

Simply put, this could well be one reason why creative writing is not something everyone does well, or that everyone seeks to do. There is something further going on here in relation to how your emotions can underpin your writerly actions. The transmission between an intensity of feeling that successfully empowers your imagination and those required formal communicative aspects of writing suggests an understanding of a particular kind. We might consider this understanding through the lens of what has been called 'Emotional Intelligence'.

Emotional Intelligence (EI) is a term coined in the early 1960s and used to describe a person's ability to recognize emotions in themselves and in others; then to use that information to guide their responses and actions. EI testing, which considers such things as self-awareness and empathy, has been posed as a behaviorally more attuned measure than Intelligence Quotient (IQ) testing, in that it is said to rate characteristics that better predict a person's leadership abilities and potential for occupational and social success. Originating in the early twentieth century, IQ testing is said to be more abstract, and to falsify the nature of intelligence by ranking characteristics of it in ascending order. Stephen Jay Gould questions these elements in his *The Mismeasure of Man* (1981).

The most well-known exploration of Emotional Intelligence is Daniel Goleman's 1995 book *Emotional Intelligence: Why It Can Matter More Than IQ*, and EI does seem to offer much for considering that creative writer's transmission between an intensity of feeling and the formal communicative aspects of writing. And yet, the word 'emotional' also defines a state in which someone's emotions are heightened, and it likewise defines a person who is prone to outbursts of emotion. Neither of these things are what you are seeking in transmission of your feelings to an understanding of emotions, and the transmission of this understanding of your emotions and those of your potential reader or audience to your work or works of creative writing.

The concept of Emotional Intelligence offers a starting point for approaching a pre- or post- event analysis of whether you are capable of understanding emotions and applying that understanding to your creative writing. Further though, what occurs in such writing is not only evidence of your Emotional Intelligence, it is most accurately the application of your Emotive Intelligence. The word 'emotive' concerns your expression of emotion. It is also referring to your ability to appeal to the emotions. Your creative writing, if it is to communicate with an audience beyond yourself, certainly involves the understanding of your emotions and those of others – and in that sense it does relate to your Emotional Intelligence. However, the event of such writing involves actions that are about expression, and specifically about using written language in a way that is distinctive in employing the heightened feelings required to make the imagination function. Emotive Intelligence is in this way directed and action-based Emotional Intelligence. It is, like all creative writing that seeks an audience, also concerned with the performative. Emotive Intelligence is the active informing of the performative event of creative writing, so that the applied understanding impacts on your technical choices and modes of expression.

As one of the keys to successful creative writing, where your writing is seeking an audience, Emotive Intelligence involves assessing how your own feelings, and the understanding of the emotions they individually represent, can be transmitted through written language. In creative writing, it is actions and acts that you initiate, draft and revise toward completion and how these bridge between your individual expression and the feelings and understandings and feelings of others. Your Emotive Intelligence is informed by your intentions, it clearly involves action, but it is also part of your decision making and your design strategies.

Such decisions include the choice of genre, the choice of voice, the choice of location to distribute your works of creative writing; and such design strategies as how your works looks, how it sounds, how sentences and phrases function within the work, in what ways parts of it relate to each other, even to conditions and facts and things beyond the work.

Emotive Intelligence is not something only of interest to creative writers or in creative writing. Rather, it is that written language, with its agreed signs, its structures, its systemic features and rules, is not necessarily the most open or fluid medium for the heightened feeling expressed through our imaginations. To make it a viable medium for such creativity, and to give it the ability to support the imaginative, means being able to assess individual feeling and gauge how to imbue such written language with emotion. Emotive Intelligence in creative writing certainly involves language structures of grammar and word choice that are also part of spoken language; but it specifically requires our attention to how such a system of generally inscribed and distributed symbols and signs becomes a medium for the exchange of human feeling.

Emotive Value

Two things are clear. Firstly, that there is value in creative writing as a mode of expression that provides a method for you of expressing and recording your feelings as well as your ideas and observations. 'Write your heart out,' declares Joyce Carol Oates, 'never be ashamed of your subject, and of your passion for your subject' (Oates, 2003: 23). If your intention is to write for yourself, the value in your creative writing will be defined by how much you feel the practice has allowed you to express yourself and how much the work that has resulted encapsulates that expression as a result of your practice. Secondly, there is value in works of creative writing for the reader or audience if you as a creative writer have the Emotive Intelligence to enable your writing to turn your individual feelings, those personal responses that define emotions for you, into exchangeable content, exploring subjects and themes using the tools of the writing arts and reaching out to an audience that is ultimately responsive to the technical and imaginative skills you display.

It is entirely possible to satisfy both yourself and a reader or audience. These aspects are not exclusive; though, it is not unusual for a creative writer to prefer one of their works that was less warmly received to one that was widely embraced. This is because your response as a creative writer is based on the satisfaction of your individual desires and the meeting of your defined intention or intentions, combined with the pleasure gained during the creative writing itself. The reader's response is defined almost solely by their experience of the final text, almost always devoid of involvement in the creating of the work, and is related to aspects of interpretation and taste that reflect their needs and desires rather than yours. The fact that any creative writer is able to successfully bridge between personal feelings and individual experiences and those of a wider readership is testament to a degree of Emotive Intelligence, to the attractions of the imaginative and creative, and to the familiarity and comfort a great many human beings acquire with the written word. This is one reason we most often describe creative writing using both the words art *and* craft. Sometimes, as in this assessment from author of such novels as *The Floating Opera* (1956), John Barth, we emphasize other words too. 'Given the inclination and the opportunity,' Barth says, 'those with any aptitude for it at all surely hone what skills they have, in the art of writing as in any other art, craft, *skill*' (Barth, 1995: 24, my emphasis).

A craft is something involving making and skill, by definition. That skill is seen to be a manual skill, often thought of as a trade skill. Art also involves your skills, but the emphasis here is the qualities of aesthetic worth, on creative aptitude and imaginative power. The ability of art to successfully reach the emotions, through aesthetic appeal, beauty, the touching of the senses and the mind, is one way in which art is differentiated from craft. Whereas dexterity is highlighted in ideas about craft, appeal is highlighted in ideas about art. Because creative writing involves the use of common written language tools, sometimes in uncommon ways, and because it displays both your creative writer's dexterity and your ability to create something with aesthetic appeal, it thus has a dual identity.

We could therefore include in the category of 'craft' such dexterous writerly achievements as the creation, maintenance and changing of the pace of a piece of creative writing, or the selecting and molding of an image or images, or the employment of resonance, or the application of rhetorical devices such as analogy or parallelism or hyperbole, or the selection and contrasting of points of view. We could include in the category of 'art' such aesthetically appealing traits as the symmetry of a work, or the way in which a story or poem has the appearance of a compositional texture, through word choice and placement, or the harmoniousness of a scene in which exposition, description and narrative seem to support each other well, or the contrasts in character or description that give the piece variety and interest, or the stimulating appeal of a thematic focal point.

And yet, the art and craft of creative writing is not about separating its categorical aspects, art from craft, but about how these elements interact. You, as a creative writer, are the orchestrator of that interaction – the initiator and the maintainer of that interaction. Intention informs what you do, your action ensures that you do it, and if you seek to reach a reader or audience your emotional engagement, informed by the strength and extent of your Emotive Intelligence, seeks an empathy with others that is both personal and communal, an exchange between single individuals and an expression of the valuable emotional bond between humans.

Exploring Emotion

- Feeling, belief and motivation are each part of creative writing. The meaning of each helps to focus our actions as creative writers. For example, your description of a personal emotion is what is meant by 'a feeling'; while your ability to transmit personal feeling into the exploration of a recognizable emotion is what creates empathy with a reader or audience.
- Creative writing animates your feelings and thoughts and it relies on and reveals your beliefs.
- Works of creative writing that communicate with and touch others are unlikely to come about mostly through an outpouring of emotion. Written communication requires us to structure, form and organize language, and this involves intellectual skills.
- Emotive Intelligence defines our ability to act on emotional understanding. The definition of the emotive relates to the event of creative writing as we make it

happen. It is emotive intelligence in action and through action.
- The value of creative writing, both to you as a creative writer and to a reader or a member of an audience, is in a large part based in an exchange of feeling. This is an emotive value, supported by the strength of your craft and given empathetic reach by the aesthetic qualities of your art.

4

Imagination

Factual, Counterfactual, Creative

Imagine a world without imaginations. In terms of quality of life, you probably would not want to do that. In terms of your abilities, you can do it. You can do this imagining because human beings have what can be called 'higher order' imaginations. Our imaginations are able to work at a level of cognitive and creative engagement that makes us distinct as a species and provides the impetus and support for such activities as creative writing. That does not make us the only living things on the planet with the ability to propose, imagine, and create. Animals have imaginations and insects create. Birds, spiders, dolphins, mice, chimpanzees, octopuses, bees – the creative activities of other living things regularly astound us, not simply because of the creativity itself but perhaps also because we value creativity so much in ourselves. Our sometimes proprietorial sense with regard to the creative seems to stem from this fact; but, more positively, might arise not from wanting to deny the power of creativity in other living things but rather from the conflating of the concepts of creativity and of the imagination. While we can recognize and even celebrate the creativity of a spider in its building of an elaborate web, or the beauty of a bird's song, or the innovation and originality in honeybees' hives and their communal patterns of honey making, we are not so inclined to consider these things the product of an imagination. While acknowledging some form of imagination plays a role in a cat treating a ball of wool as if it is a mouse to be chased or a chimpanzee playing a game of pretend, we assess the order of imaginative input in these activities as less than that undertaken by humans. An accurate assessment in that your imagination is not only concerned with forming mental representations it is also about the workings of your mind, the extent and employment of your intelligence, and in this way our imaginations involve heightened response and considered explanation and active supposition. Our imaginations challenge, they construct, destruct, propose, and counter-propose. Imagining can be considered both an ability and a process, often combining the innate with the potential, the already present with the conceivably achievable. There are said to be different types or versions of the imagination, defined according to the ways in which these function and the reasons and aims behind their functioning.

In one example of these explorations, Colin McGinn, in his book *Mindsight: Image, Dream, Meaning* (2004), talks of imagining in terms of contrasts with perception (or 'precepts' as McGinn refers to it), explores aspects of delusion and the nature of visuality, and differentiates between 'sensory imagining' and 'cognitive imagining' (McGinn, 2004: 4). McGinn's subtitle is essentially diagnostic – *Image, Dream, Meaning* identifies visuality as the most likely component of your imagining, the kind of interpretative engagement needed with dreams as being commonly required, and the combined senses of imagining conveying something but also, in another definition of the concept of 'meaning', that this something is likely to have significance. He queries what differentiates an image from a perception, suggesting these differ in 'a number of fundamental respects' (2). In this regard, he speaks of 'the mind's eye', and suggests this kind of seeing is different from seeing with your external eyes. Therefore, to approach the imagination as if it is a version of external seeing is to falsify how imagining functions. McGinn does suggest, however, that both the mind's eye, as he refers to it, and perception are directed toward an external object (4); and in that way they share a focus on a concrete object, which may or may not be actual. The importance of an exploration such as McGinn's is that it further unwraps what mental capacities and tools we have at our disposal when undertaking creative writing. Creative writing is not, as is commonly suggested, ingenuously imaginative writing – that is, it is not merely writing in which a singular fantastical unstudied occurrence, defined as 'the imaginative', elevates its originality and simultaneously your capacity as a creative writer to wonder, speculate, investigate, explore.

McGinn's suggestion that the so-named mind's eye is focusing on something concrete, real or otherwise, is itself a challenge to the way in which creative writing is oftentimes perceived, where invention and originality are seen to be dependent on a kind of otherworldliness that only those uniquely capable of transcendental transference are capable of approaching. Rather, your imagining deals in the concrete and it is not in this sense in opposition to the factual, the actual. Your imagining also seeks both to grasp and to speculate, and there are a variety of circumstances, reasons, and outcomes projected by different types of imagining. The type most often referred to, generically, when talking about creative writing is what has been called 'creative thought' or the 'creative imagination' but will be called here the 'inventive imagination' to emphasize the elements of formation, of first time creation. Ruth Byrne notes that 'creative thoughts are relied upon to write a poem, paint a picture, compose a piece of music, design an experiment, or invent a new product' (451), but also that 'these sorts of activities can seem very different from the imagination of a counterfactual alternative to reality' (451–452).

The 'counterfactual imagination', Byrne continues, 'is one sort of imaginative thought' (452). In that instance, she writes, 'people consider two possibilities when they understand the counterfactual, the imagined possibility' (450). Most significantly, Byrne argues that our imaginations can be rational. She offers more on this in her book *The Rational Imagination: How People Create Alternatives to Reality* (2005). A rational imagination producing counterfactual thoughts – this idea is not necessarily directly opposed to the widely held, generic version of the imagination that pervades much thought and discussion about creative writing. The imagination, as it influences creative writing, has often been viewed as an organizing force, and therefore not entirely irrational. However, such a suggestion that imagining can be rational is much more directed toward critical application than the generic view of the creative writing imagination, and points to the plausibility of an elevation in originality and inventiveness not being otherworldly; but, instead, being the result of having developed your critical understanding as well as the influence of inspired vision.

What we have here, in these examples from McGinn and Byrne, just two of a number of scholars of the imagination, is a picture of our imagining that depicts it as multidimensional, frequently purposeful, and certainly not solely concerned with the fantastical. It is also not a detached capacity, something that operates independently of your other cognitive functions. Your general ability to imagine involves patterns of thinking, accessing memory, applying knowledge, that are shared, much as Byrne also suggests in the specific counterfactual instance that 'counterfactual imaginative thoughts share some similarities with other sorts of creative thoughts, such as category expansion, concept combination, and insight' (451).

With such explorations of human imagining in mind, we can best understand the imagination as we employ it for creative writing in three intersecting and interacting *ways*, involving these three intersecting and interacting *aspects*:

The **factual** – Your imagining drawing on your knowledge of events, activities, people, things, employing insights that are drawn from previous sensory experiences, that uses your mind to *re*-experience these events, activities, people, things, even though they are not immediately available to you via your senses.

The **counterfactual** – Your imagining proposing an alternative to the factual view of events, activities, people, things. This counterfactual view, while alternative is still plausible and you engage it in order to consider 'what if' questions, those speculative examinations that assist you in confirming or challenging fact, proposing scenarios or outcomes that are more satisfying or pleasurable than those that would be considered true.

The **inventive** – Your imagining of the extraordinary, its formation, not necessarily abandoning fact or counter-fact but without the necessity of a grounding in that fact or rational counter-fact. Speculative, fanciful, or abstracted. Your imagining, while capable of being directed toward concrete, external objects, as McGinn describes, here is potentially being shaped by your mind alone.

Your human imagination is of a high order because of the depth and breadth of our human cognition. As a species, we do not uniquely possess imaginations, and we do not uniquely create; however, we do uniquely use our imaginations in such heightened and sometimes transcendental ways to extend our engagement with the world we have experienced and all that we have not experienced but can be speculative upon; to create art; to explore and develop knowledge; and to strengthen our communication with each other. Fiction writer, critic, and philosophy professor William Gass says: 'above all, I believe consciousness is the residence and nurturing place of the imagination' (Gass, 1996: 41), referring clearly to the consciousness of humans. He goes on:

> Without impudent comparisons, without freewheeling, without dreams, without invention, without the transformation of metaphor, the burglary of meaning that symbols commit: without such aeration, prose deflates, our tires turn on air; flat, they leave their rubber on the highway; but, in

addition, the other elements of a good sentence – desire, feeling, sensation, thought – require the imagination for their construction. (Gass, 1996: 41)

In creative writing our capacity, ability, and frequently also our willingness and sense of support for our communication between the factual, counterfactual, and inventive imagination are grounded in the fact we are using written language (the 'using' referring to the 'construction' Gass mentions), and empowered by the desire to make that written language aesthetically pleasing as well as functional, emotionally engaging, and informative, personal, and communal.

Mental Representations

The word declares it; the ancient origins of the word seem to confirm the declaration: that the 'imagination' is concerned with the creation of images. Conceptual, or drawn from memory, or fanciful, or drawn from supposition, conjecture or speculation, complex or simple, in all cases images. 'Images', while also used to generally refer to mental entities, most strongly refers to the visual. Definitions have a strong element of truth because they are agreed shorthand forms of commonsense communication. Yet clearly a definition that suggests your imagination deals only in the visual is incorrect. Colloquially we make that plain.

'Imagine what that *sounds* like.' 'Can you imagine what that *feels* like?' When we speak of the imagination, as when we employ the imagination, what we are actually producing is not solely mental pictures. What we are producing is mental representations. These representations brought to life by your imagination might of course be visual – but they might be auditory, or they might be olfactory, or tactile. Frequently these mental representations are a combination of such sensory information, *re*-produced or produced in your mind. In your mind (though not limited to what Colin McGinn calls 'the mind's 'eye'; as McGinn agrees and thus also refers to 'the mind's ear' [McGinn: 77]) mental representations take on the character of their perceived external counterparts, manifestations of concrete real or unreal entities. Because in creative writing your imagination can combine the factual, the counterfactual, and the inventive, such representations can also contain elements of each or all of these.

In approaching your imaginative representations in creative writing you can consider process, the subject, and the overall content. Your process includes the investigative nature of what you do – how you find out; the knowledge you possess; the way you ascertain what is fact and what is not fact, your comparing and contrasting, using such things as parallelism, analogy, metaphor, correspondence and coherence as guides to your processing of observations, memories, deduction, and induction; moving from specific instances to general principles, from general principles to specific applications. All of this making sense of your experiences is supporting you in such personal sense making, as well as assisting you in creating theories and hypotheses that might be personalized or have wider application, relevance, or grounding.

Your imagining as a process relies on the language of categorizing and of organizing, creating sequences and relationships between what and when and who – what space, time, and order you imagine them. Imagining in this sense relies on both your personal psychology and your social and cultural background. Combined, the knowledge you have and the understanding you apply to the process are as influential as your specific subject matter and as the overall content of your imagining, surrounding that subject.

To give an example of how this works, consider that you imagine a scene in a city street and it plays out with a focus on two young men playing acoustic guitars, busking on the steps of a city library with an imposing gothic façade, while in the park, across the street, a preschool group is accompanied by parents, mostly young mothers, on swings and an elaborate plastic playset of a fantasy castle and colorful slides and tunnels, bright yellow, bright green, bright red, as along the paths of the park the street workers from the city pace through, joggers pass, the two young men grow louder, a song you recognize but can't seem to name, and a taxi pulls up at the curb, and is a yellow cab like the kind you once slipped into, once, in New York, but it is not New York, even though the driver looks exactly like the driver you remember in New York, and there is thunder or maybe it is the sound of the semi truck you see now passing on the street way beyond the park, one of those that used to carry sand from the back of the beach where you once lived, and out of the taxi there's another young man stepping onto the steps, but lower down now, the two men playing guitars noticing him, and the contrast between him and them, the arriving man in his dark gray suit, the two young men in jeans and flowing colorful shirts, now shirts that appear to have taken on the colors of the playset in the park, and the passersby on the street now seem to have all but disappeared as the library grows taller from the angle of the street below and the subject which is now the man ascending the stairs is seen from the point of view of the guitar players, who have now stopped playing and are watching as the children from the park begin running up the stairs, passing the man from the cab who is arranging a black coat on his arm, shouldering his black carrier bag, now looking up toward them, now pausing, staring.

This scene, which you imagine, in sights, sounds, the smells of the city street, the feel of the hard marble steps of the library, the slick plastic surfaces of the slides, the sequence of movements in the street, beyond the street, close by on the library, shifting viewpoints from the guitar players to the wider park view to the street view to the view of the arriving taxi, momentarily then among the ascending children, for a split second back at the beach where you grew up, then on the hard marble steps, then by the side of a path in the park, then up beside the library's doors, the imposing columns beside you, the runnels of these, the height of the building, darkly shadowing the entrance, all this is ordered and related and placed in parallel and juxtaposition and contrast and comparison and processed as your imagining of a scene in which three college friends meet for the first time in a few years, friends who have found themselves taking different directions, but carrying with them a version of an innocent event from their college years that, here in the moment of their reacquaintance, is to take on unprecedented significance.

Subject, content, and process are all interactively at work in your imagining. Images are created and recreated, and because images are naturally and considerably generative – that is, they produce descendent images, offshoots, seed further images – one image potentially generates and supports a range of others. Other sensory information, based on your past experiences, your knowledge and understanding, informs and is encapsulated in your imaginative explorations. This also influences and directs your creative decisions, how you initiate, design, and conduct your imagining. Psychologically, you are further selecting and arranging, drawing on memory, you are applying personal 'what if' principles in reworking sensory information, creating from feeling elements in your imagining, elements that might or might not be real but that refer to projected concrete entities beyond your mind.

When imagining you are also using common organizational entities and principles, those with which you are familiar because they are drawn from the world in which you live. These are such entities and principles as structure, form, function, and system. Such entities and principles are evident to you in literal and metaphoric ways, being as connected to you as the structure and function and systemic nature of your own body and mind and as separate from you, yet still known, as aspects of geography, the compositional qualities of varieties of substances and forms, the different kinds of actions and movements, and the relationship of things and activities in their individual occupying of time and space. So while your inventive imagination might indeed create the improbable or the fantastical, in creative writing you are also utilizing factual and counterfactual imagining. And all your imagining, in all its guises, is informed by your personal, societal, and cultural influences, as well as historical and contemporary contexts.

Your imagination also draws on how you create and how you construct meaning. Your imagining can therefore include connotative elements – in other words, elements where the meaning is implied or suggested. In the city scene, for example, the colors, the presence of ominous, thunderous sound, the group of children, the imposing city library, all are imaginative explorations in connotative meaning. Your imagination can also denote, such denotation dealing in direct meaning. Imagining as mental representation can portray – portraying suggests describing, showing, acting out. Imagining can also offer signs and symbols, representing ideas, beliefs, or feelings, combining these perhaps. A sign tends to denote, be directly informational, relatively conventional in its meaning, and relate to conscious action and observable entities. A symbol, however, works more by association and suggestion, draws from your unconscious, and is complex and often multidimensional in meaning.

Standing for something or somethings, and the result of your learned understanding rather than instinctive, symbols have a marked ability to evoke feeling. They reflect your imagination's dependence on heightened feeling, a level of cognitive and creative engagement that allows you to construct and experience things and activities that are not actually present. And symbols are not limited to literal planes of reference. They can be allusive, they can be provocative, and they can be equivocal. While your imagining might construct and present signs, and thus direct and widely agreed representational elements, it also deals in symbols, and in doing so is the site not only of publicly highly recognizable representations, but also of personal symbolic references, entities which you as the person imagining are more attuned with, more engaged with emotionally or intellectually.

Your imagination, when applied to communication tasks, such as the art and craft of creative writing, needs to be able to employ in both a personal and public way the elevated sense of emotive engagement that is core to imagining, creating connections and associations, to provide for the transmitting of thoughts, ideas, observations, emotions. Like language and symbols, the power of the mental representations of your imagining to do that is a learned ability with which each of us can engage.

Developing Your Imagination

Because your imagination is a mental ability, it makes sense that developing your mental abilities will assist you in developing your imagination. However, imagining is a particular ability and process with particular functions, reasons, and aims. In Jean-Paul Sartre's childhood memoir *Words* he writes:

> Through my flights of imagination, I was trying to attain reality. When my mother asked me, without looking away from her music: 'Poulou, what are you doing?' I would sometimes break my vow of silence and answer: 'I'm making films.' In fact, I was trying to tear ideas from my mind and bring them to life outside myself, amidst real furniture and real walls, as bright and as clear as the ones which flowed on the screen. (Sartre,1967: 90)

Everyone possesses an imagination; however, not everyone possesses the same imaginative capacities. With this in mind, having a strong mental capacity clearly does not inevitably mean you have an active and robust imagination. A number of factors appear to have major roles in taking what is one of our innate human traits and making it more prominent, more constructive, more dynamic in each of us. Whether factual, counterfactual, or inventive your capacity for imagining can firstly be gauged, and it can be potentially enhanced, with attention to the following areas:

> Your **curiosity** – Is associated with seeking, and it is most often considered something we (and other animals) do and develop with the aim of gaining knowledge. This information-based interpretation of curiosity points you toward the notion that your imagination can benefit from understanding and from the seeking of understanding. This appears to be true. However, it masks an additional aspect that we can call 'affective curiosity' – an aspect present in human curiosity. Affective, meaning associated with your feelings and emotions. Affective curiosity is thus when we seek experiences that are purported to provide certain emotional stimuli, to have an influence on our feelings. Theories about consumerism and our consumption of material goods and services have talked about the role of emotional connection, desire, and satisfaction in our purchasing. Consumerism is dependent on this cycle involving desire, gaining of satisfaction through consuming, new desire. Here too is an example of affective curiosity. We hear a particular new model car is 'exhilarating' to drive or a brand of toothpaste makes your teeth feel particularly 'fresh' or a visit to a tourist attraction is 'fascinating' and we are not curious (in the first two instances, certainly) about the new knowledge that will be provided. Rather, we are curious about the feelings that might be initiated, most obviously in relation to pleasure.

Your curiosity, therefore, is both about understanding and about feeling, particularly feelings of pleasure. Developing your curiosity provides fuel for your motivations and for your actions. To be curious means seeking out new knowledge, new feelings, new understanding, new pleasures. How you do this will be determined by your personal preferences and your cultural situation, but doing it is undoubtedly part of further developing your imagination.

Newness – Is associated with both imagining and creativity. This is so in the case of the imagination because the suggestion, or at very least the inference, is that the mental representations that are formed by imagining have not been formed previously. If they have been formed previously they might, alternatively, be considered to be part of your memory. So newness plays a role in imagining – even when that newness involves a revision of previously imagined entities or events. In the case of creativity, newness is associated with concepts such as invention and innovation, often seen as synonyms for creativity or components of it. Something new comes about because of creativity, whether that newness contributes to tangible or intangible entities. For example, an idea can be new and so can a painting.

Identifying newness involves knowledge of what has come before and of what currently exists. This is not as simple a statement as it appears. Each of us exists within the parameters of limited space and time. While the contemporary world has in some ways expanded for us through the invention and impact of virtual worlds, social media technologies, digital connectivity, and a myriad of communication and knowledge technologies that have extended our reach and our access to knowledge and experiences, we as individuals and as members of particular social groups are still limited by our capacity to discover, consider, and apply newness. Even if we were not influenced by prevailing paradigms and archetypes, even if we were not creatures who form and maintain habits, even if we were not influenced by established social conventions, our latitude for finding and applying aspects of newness is limited by our ability to discover all that is currently or has been discovered or created.

Thus newness is a component of both creativity and the imagination, but our ability to discover genuine newness and apply it to our creative writing is one of our greatest of challenges. This is exacerbated by the fact that writing generally relies on conventions, and that without many of those conventions, that minimizing of uniqueness, written communication would be unintelligible. Therefore, as creative writers our language tools are often ordinary while our imaginative needs are frequently extraordinary. To further explore newness we can do such things as delve into specific fields of knowledge, increasing our awareness of those particular knowledge domains; we can access historical and alternative cultural differences and apply them to contemporary and/or our known cultural conditions; we can find newness in viewpoint or voice, whereas your imaginative contribution is to see and relate things from a different angle; we can explore imaginative newness in our personal histories, which can bring to a topic an observation or a belief in the uniqueness of our individual personalities; we can also promote newness through shifting the plane of reference, shifting from one plane of reference to another in the way of metaphor, where characteristics of something are transferred to something else.

Planes of Reference – Departing from the literal, newness can be produced through the metaphoric associating of something with something else. Such a shift in the plane of reference produces depth of investigation, a way of expanding and intensifying our creative explorations. This figurative associating might be as concentrated as writing that there was a 'blanket' of snow or that a certain workplace was a 'zoo' or that the 'barbs' of a character's wit produced physical reactions. Such concentrated metaphor works as a device to deepen an observation, a point made, a reference. Elseways, a metaphor might extend to detailed figurative mapping, where the way something else looks or behaves forms the underpinning of your literal focus, and this figurative plane offers the opportunity for parallelism, for creating supportive narrative, for adding examinations that delve into forms or attitudes or characteristics by exploring the identical aspects on another plane of reference, and in this way giving further dimensional extent to that on the literal plane. Sometimes we refer to these more extended figurative explorations as allegories or parables.

Written metaphors – and not all metaphors are written, of course; visual metaphors are common too, and musical metaphors of movement and motion assist in shaping music – like all metaphors, utilize analogy. This analogical mode of engaging with ideas, thoughts, observations, which is also seen in similes, contributes to explanation and assists in suggesting solutions to problems. It's a mode of engagement that extends your cognitive function through association and correspondence, and in the way of the rhetorical use, also suggests opposites: disassociation and contrast. Metaphor's analogical mode can be allusive and largely implied. Or it can be unambiguous, even blunt.

A metaphor can work heuristically so that it draws a reader or audience or indeed you as creative writer to new discoveries, new understandings. It can appear to offer proof for a thought or suggestion by the fluency of their association with your literal focus or by appealing to points of recognition, even though that recognition is associated with depictions on another plane of reference altogether – for example, pointing to the savagery and expansiveness of a stormy sea as depicting the savagery and length of a military battle, even though the physical characteristics, and the comparison of space and time, would otherwise suggest difference not sameness. Such analogy as deployed in metaphor, and in simile too, conceives and creates. Metaphors stimulate thought as much as they organize thoughts, and they assist in building your confidence in perception and analysis because they purport to offer evidence for your ways of thinking. Your imagination, powering your creative writing, gains from this figurative realm not only in sourcing content or in organizing that content but also through what can be called the meta condition of the shifting plane of reference from the 'page' where your creative writing is being brought into existence to the concrete entities beyond the page to which your creative writing is referring or addressing or bringing to life.

Play – Do you have to be good at play to be good at creative writing? It is a question that targets the significance of such writing as a social and cultural activity as well as its relevance to your personal daily life. Further, it is a question that can be broadened to a consideration of the significance of the arts to humankind generally. Nobel Prize winner Günter Grass includes play in his description of finding a way of writing his novel *The Tin Drum* (1959):

> With the first sentence – 'Granted: I am an inmate of a mental hospital … ' – my block was gone, words pressed in on me, memory, imagination, playfulness, and obsession with detail gave themselves free rein, chapter engendered chapter. (Grass: 1985: 27)

Of course, as with the imagination, play is also not limited to human beings. We observe many instances of animal play, which is perhaps a good indication that play is often other than whimsical behavior. Our human imaginations are associated with play that often involves the 'pretend' or 'make-believe', when referring to children and childhoods. All this grounds play in such things as our rehearsing for real situations – we see this in any number of childhood games, or indeed in the 'play' fighting between animals – to cognitive growth, whereby thinking and then acting out scenarios and imitating and exploring alternative viewpoints or ways of behaving enhances our thinking process, and access to our feelings and our understanding of emotions. Play is certainly often fun, but it is far from always frivolous. Play can ground personal identity in group activities and perspectives, and provide a guide to how you maneuver and work within defined time and space. Play can be a consideration of the rules of interaction with others and a challenge to how we can relate one human perspective to another.

There are therefore many reasons to believe that the answer to the question 'Do you have to be good at play to be good at creative writing?' is 'yes'. Even the simple suggestion to 'play regularly with words and ideas' in order to improve your imagining is well-supported by such evidence as the ways in which we learn social rules through play and the ways in which we rehearse interpretations of the world through play. Play gives your imagination somewhere to experiment and, in doing so, empowers improvement in your imagining, capitalizing on and ultimately enhancing your capacities.

Figuration – Because your imagination deals in the shaping of figures, with instances of the metaphoric and the analogical, your attention to figuration underscores the making you are engaged in, the role of your imagining in creating something anew. Figuration means the creating of a representation, something that illustrates, something shaped. Figuration also suggests the emblematic or symbolic, and we know our imaginations frequently use symbols. Your figuration involves design, and designing has intention. The role of intention in creative writing makes figuration a natural fit with this specific kind of writing where intention and action are so informed and guided by the imagination, often incorporating your feelings in an interaction at both a content and emotional level with others in the world.

Figuration in music refers to a short succession of notes, repeated and giving an impression of some kind, and we can think of figuration by your imagination in a similar way. It is your creation of a shape to your creative writing whereby your imagining creates motifs and characteristics that return in the same or resonant forms throughout the piece, that guide you and guide your reader or audience toward a meaning or meanings.

Interaction – Toward the end of the twentieth century we entered a period of history, most certainly in the developed world, strongly influenced by contemporary digital technologies. These technologies include the mobile phone and computers connected to the internet, technologies that have been used to increase the breadth and reach of human exchanges. Whether in the context of an exchange of professional or commercial content and information or for social purposes, contemporary digital technologies have changed the intensity, conditions, and indeed use of such concepts as connectivity, networking, and interaction. These concepts have had earlier existences; the idea of a network, for example, has origins as long ago as the sixteenth century where it related to the intersecting of threads or wires. But the contemporary world has redoubled our discussion of and interest in connectivity, networking, and interaction. One thing this redoubling does is to remind us of how much our use of our imaginations in our creative writing aims to create interaction.

Interaction is about influencing or doing things with others. While it might be said that your imagination is not doing things with others if you are only writing for yourself, in fact your imagination is already culturally and socially informed as well as a product of your own mind. Imaginations are interactive by virtue of their outward-facing creativity. By nature, your imagination interacts, in that sense; and where your creative writing is produced in terms of communication with others you further seek interaction in the form of influencing your reader or audience. This influence is not only informational but also emotional. Interaction is also about reciprocity, and we see many references to this in reference to 'writing for a reader' or similar expressions that attempt to explain the nature of interpersonal communication in and through creative writing.

In reality, reciprocity in creative writing is not 'writing for a reader'. Rather it is more accurately understood as establishing and developing how your imagination shares meaning. How such imagining structures and organizes the literal and the figurative to explore, articulate, and exchange experiences with others. And how it grounds things and activities created in your mind in concrete entities and actions that others can recognize or with which they can feel association. Considering and engaging with how you create interactions means being aware of the signs and symbols you are employing. It means your patterning of denotative and connotative meaning. It involves the heightening of feeling in others brought about by your own heightened imaginative state. Finally, interaction as part of your imagining entails you categorizing and organizing the sequence of the subject matter with which you are dealing so that the personal influences these contain are grounded in factual, counterfactual, or inventive patterns that support the desires of your reader or audience when experiencing your work.

Exploring Imagination

- There is not one imagination but many – and not only in the sense that your own is highly individual, distinctively part of who you are as well as showing the influence of your society and culture. Types of imagining influence and inform your creative writing and those types can be defined and considered when composing a piece of work.
- Human imagining is of a high order – informed by the extent of your knowledge and understanding as well as by the extent of your creativity. The imagination, while an innate quality, is not innately powerful or productive – that comes about through learning and is improved by use and application.
- Signs and symbols are the crux of imagination, and their relationships and ordering are the foundation on which all imaginative explorations are built.
- It is almost impossible to create something new without having curiosity and it is equally difficult to initiate newness without an element of play.
- The figurative works in your creative writing to deepen understanding and to create the potential for stronger human interactions. It does so because to shift the plane of reference increases the number of possible points of connection, recognition, or emotional engagement, both yours as a creative writer and those of any reader or audience.

5

Pleasure

'Suffering is Optional'

The eminent writer Joyce Carol Oates writes in *The Faith of a Writer: Life, Craft and Art* (2004), forty years after she published the first of her many novels:

> The practicing writer, the writer-at-work, the writer immersed in his or her project, is not an entity at all, let alone a person, but a curious mélange of wildly varying states of mind, clustered toward what might be called the darker end of the spectrum: indecision, frustration, pain, dismay, despair, remorse, impatience, outright complete failure. (Oates, 2004: 51–52)

Oates is not the first, and certainly not the only creative writer to speak of what she calls 'the darker end of the spectrum'. Author of the award-winning novel *The Wind-Up Bird Chronicle*, among many other works, Haruki

Murakami, in his *What I Talk About When I Talk About Running* (2008), his title reflecting Raymond Carver's short story collection *What We Talk About When We Talk About Love* (1981), portrays the analogous heavy, aching struggles of marathon running and creative writing. In his Foreword, entitled 'Suffering is Optional', Murakami writes:

> Writers who are blessed with inborn talent can freely write novels no matter what they do – or don't do. Like water from a natural spring, the sentences just well up, and with little or no effort these writers can complete a work. Occasionally you'll find someone like that, but, unfortunately, that category wouldn't include me. I haven't spotted any springs nearby. I have to pound the rock with a chisel and dig out a deep hole before I can locate the source of creativity. To write a novel I have to drive myself hard physically and use a lot of time and effort. Every time I begin a new novel, I have to dredge out another new, deep hole. (Murakami, 2008: 43)

'I have to pound the rock with a chisel and dig out a deep hole before I can locate the source of creativity' – Murakami's description, the hefty labor, the pain, the malefic darkness of his activity of creative writing, maps directly on to Oates's 'indecision, frustration, pain, dismay, despair, remorse, impatience, outright complete failure'. These responses, which again to note here are far from unique, raise the seemingly simplistic but not entirely facetious question: Why would *anyone* want to do this creative writing thing?

If what Joyce Carol Oates and Haruki Murakami say is true, then what you enjoy about creative writing is balanced by the pain of you doing it. If such writing provides you with gratification, then, following that pattern, it is matched by a degree of woe. If such writing makes you pleased, then it equally makes you displeased. Finally, if you have a desire to do it, you also have a desire not to be doing it.

The seeming paradox of creative writing has long been commented upon and has manifested itself in an effort both by creative writers and by critics who are not creative writers to come to terms with what it is that the practice of creative writing actually entails – beyond the presence and development of technical writing skills, that is. Often that effort of discovery focuses on the emotional, intellectual, and physical intensity of the practice. Rainer Maria Rilke, in *Letters to a Young Poet* (1934; first published in German as *Briefe an einen jungen Dichter* in 1929 and consisting of letters written by Rilke to the young poet of the title, Franz Xaver Kappus, between 1902 and 1908), adds to a theme of difficulty the themes of aloneness and solitude – particularly referencing the spiritual and the psychological:

> Nobody can counsel and help you, nobody. There is only one single way. Go into yourself. Search for the reason that bids you write; find out whether it is spreading out its roots in the deepest places of your heart, acknowledge to yourself whether you would have to die if it were denied you to write. This above all – ask yourself in the stillest hour of your night: *must* I write? And if this should be affirmative, if you may meet this earnest question with a strong and simple '*I must*', then build your life according to this necessity; your life even into its most indifferent and slightest hour must be a sign of this urge and a testimony to it. (Rilke, 1934: 18–19)

Rilke additionally gives us here the common creative writing theme of the imperative. Write because you answer 'Yes' to the question '*must* I write?' Write because 'you would have to die if it were denied you to write'. Your undertaking of creative writing is urgent, vital, and crucial – to you. If this is indeed the case, and assuming it is so because it is in some way indispensable to you, then consider what pleasures creative writing might bring you, taking pleasure to be firstly the more simple notion of enjoyment. What enjoyment do you find in creative writing, and therefore what things might you do to further develop your writing by focusing on these points of enjoyment?

A **physical** practice. The sweep of the quill, the scrape of a pencil, the pressing of keys on a typewriter, the speaking into a Dictaphone – throughout history there have been many choices of how a creative writer might physically convert their thoughts and feelings into inscribed creative text. The physicality of creative writing is related not only to its past history, where doing it necessarily involved low to moderate physical action, but also to the contemporary world where its corporeal nature is less, but not gone. The impression of creative writing being a craft, and therefore involving manual dexterity, and the fact it only comes about through forms of action, makes this so. While it would be stretching the point to suggest that your writing often involves you raising a sweat, it would be wrong for us to ignore this physical nature. Creative writing might not be the kind of activity that regularly increases your endorphin levels or produces in you higher amounts of dopamine, serotonin, and norepinephrine, the byproducts of exercise and all of which are associated with an increase in happiness. But the physical actions of writing are a confirmation for you that you are in some sense progressing toward a projected goal, in some sense satisfying your desire to write creatively. They give you pleasure. Much else might occur to complicate your passage toward your goal, but the physicality of you undertaking the writing gives you a sense of control, generates a transferable vitality, and creates a connection between your feelings and thoughts and the personal action that consequently energizes you.

The quality of **expressiveness** is a significant contributor to the enjoyment you gain from your creative writing. That is, creative writing is a unique form of written communication in its combining of forms of knowledge and creativity in such a way as to intersect these naturally, patterning them via its methods and techniques in a manner defined by traditions and contemporary conditions of a particular creative writing genre, but equally available to your interpretation and personal inventiveness. While creatively writing you are employing your imagination as a guiding structural, formal, and systemic force that distinguishes the attributes of your creative writing from other forms of writing. Such manifest expressiveness ensures an increased meaningfulness for you, and this is part of your enjoyment, part of the pleasure.

Creative writing is a **language art**. The origins of human language, and later of written communication, reveal a story of both human need and human want. We humans needed to communicate in order to live on a planet not always easily understood, to seek out ways of engaging successfully with other humans on the basis of seeking or possessing resources, some scarce, some abundant, to establish roles, to implement and further individual and groups goals, to meet needs and to pursue wants. The complexity and range of human language is remarkable. We can express or we can query, present or solicit, and the combinations of linguistic units at our disposal are almost limitless. Yet, in our daily lives, in those common verbal or written interactions that are habitual and frequently expedient, we use only a small portion of language. Your creative writing therefore provides an avenue for your exploration and development of your somewhat underutilized language. It is a platform for those with a love of language, and provides a degree of perpetuation by that language use being in written form. Because we human beings have evolved into such sophisticated and eager language users, it makes sense that we would gain pleasure from exhibiting language skills and from extending our abilities. Gaining satisfaction from this does not of course mean needing to use language in a strange, esoteric, or enigmatic manner – though some might say that compared to day-to-day use some works of creative writing do that. Generally, however, the satisfaction comes from more fully utilizing what we have or would by our creative actions advance. It is a satisfaction gained in cultivating and in seeing human language flourish.

Empathetic communication. If works of creative writing are intended to reach and communicate with others, and a vast number of them are, then they are dependent on the creation of synaptic points of contact and transfer whereby not only information is transported between you, the creative writer, and others but also feelings, emotional context, and perceptions, together with personal interests, beliefs, attitudes, interpretations, and even your expectations. This does not mean that creative writers are by nature more empathetic than anyone else; that they are people who in science fiction have sometimes been called 'empaths'. Rather, it means that successful works of creative writing are examples of empathetic communication, the creative writer succeeding in showing in them an awareness of the thoughts and feelings of others – whether on the exterior of the writing, where there is an explicit reference and articulation of such thoughts or feelings, or implicitly where a work is imbued with that empathetic connective quality through its themes and subjects, viewpoints, voices, and tone. Because we humans have the capacity to be empathetic, to respond to the feelings of others, to group together through a mirroring of the thoughts and attitudes of those around us in the world, empathetic communication is a reference to a shared existence and the pleasure gained from that, from a sense of not being alone, is another contribution to our attraction to creative writing.

Cultural significance (also incorporating a celebration of talent). Creative writing is culturally revered – admittedly not in all its forms or in all its genres to the same extent, or by all people equally or by everyone for the same reasons. Predominantly, nevertheless, the practice of writing creatively is recognized as a distinguished contributor to culture, and as a notable recorder and repository of human experiences and outlooks. Works of creative writing that are critically judged to be significant are further held up as achievements that reflect on the capacity of humankind to make art, and those who create such works are frequently revered for their talent. This public celebration of works of creative writing reflects positively on the occupation of being a creative writer and provides an aspirational quality to the practice that is both personally challenging and enlivening. Not everyone might want to be a famous writer, but the recognition of the talent involved in being good at creative writing is nevertheless a component of the personal desire to attempt to do it. Such recognition of ability generates confidence, a sense of reward that counters such negative feelings as anxiety, skepticism, powerlessness. Participating in a culturally significant practice with the opportunity of reward is thus undoubtedly a motivator, if not for all creative writers then at least for some.

Finally, together with its potential to display and exemplify empathy, one human being recognizing the perspectives of another, by **making the ordinary extraordinary**, creative writing furthermore supports individuality, uniqueness, the role of the self in society and in sense making. Your creative writing is therefore one way in which you are making sense of things happening to you and events occurring around you. It provides a way of making meaning, considering and organizing what you observe, as well as what you believe you have come to understand. Because creative writing is so multifaceted, this sense making or meaning making has the power to affect you in a range of responses. These can be as varied as your reasoned processing of your observations to determine their veracity, to your visceral reactions that are less about reason and more about what is most often called 'instinct'. That creative writing is acknowledged for appreciating the innate as well as the learned, the intuitive as well as the mediated, the spontaneous as well as the deliberate, it promotes a holistic sense of the self – and by doing this, gives you the pleasure of completeness that other forms of communication and representation do not always offer.

A physical activity, promoting and developing expressiveness, as a written language art, featuring empathetic communication, being of cultural significance, and making the ordinary extraordinary, all would seem good reasons to consider that creative writing can bring you, the creative writer, pleasure. However, this has not answered the question clearly posed by the statements of Joyce Carol Oates and Haruki Murakami, among many other creative writers who, speaking from considerable personal experience, suggest that creative writing is not solely pleasure; it also is pain.

So, is suffering optional?

There are a number of ways we might respond to this question. Firstly, it might be that creative writing simply is painful. Why we do it, then, is largely a mystery – though our reasoning might be connected to such things as our strong desire for expressiveness, our evolutionary engagement with language, and our belief that creative writing is culturally significant. Secondly, it might be that Oates and Murakami are exaggerating and that the pleasure gained from creative writing usually outweighs any pain any of us might experience when doing it. This could perhaps be mediated by how often such writing meets your expectations, satisfies your intentions. The pain exists, therefore, but is made less or is even negated by the joy of accomplishment – which, by that measure, could perhaps result also in making your unsuccessful moments of creative writing more painful. Thirdly, it might be that certain aspects of creative writing are painful and certain aspects are pleasurable and that you have to endure the painful portions in order to get to the pleasurable ones. Finally, it might be that while we have long reported the difficulty, the labor, the intensity of the experience of such writing we have also long misinterpreted how this relates to an informed understanding of pleasure. In essence, it might be that we misunderstand how pleasure occurs, as well as pain's possible role in it.

Generally, pleasure is seen as being at the opposite end of a spectrum to pain or is viewed as an alternate sensation, not on a spectrum but as something entirely different. Clearly, on this basis, with pleasure being pleasurable and pain being painful, you might be expected to always move toward the former and move away from the latter. However, whether on a spectrum or scale, or viewed as a separate, opposing sensation, the relationship between pleasure and pain is not such a simple one. For example, Paul Rozin and colleagues have proposed that what they call 'hedonic reversals' are a 'major source of pleasure', and they incorporate these findings into their theory of 'benign masochism' (Rozin et al., 2013: 439):

> Benign masochism refers to enjoying initially negative experiences that the body (brain) falsely interprets as threatening. This realization that the body has been fooled, and that there is no real danger, leads to pleasure derived from 'mind over body'. (Rozin et al., 2013: 439)

Together with his colleagues Rozin, a psychologist who . . . has also written on pleasure in human responses to food and to music, as well as publishing several works about the nature and practice of disgust, thus gives us the notion of forms of pleasure brought about by 'mind over body'. Having emphasized creative writing as a physical activity, as well as an activity of the mind, the theory of 'benign masochism' might well be a contribution to explaining comments such as those of Oates and Murakami. It could be conceivable. Further, we can talk about neurological conditions, the operations of our individual nervous systems, perceptions of pleasure and pain that are attached to your ideas of reward and of punishment. We can investigate degrees of pleasure and degrees of pain, or discuss the relationships between sensation and our individual interpretations of sensation.

All these responses to pleasure are individual, part of your identity, as well as part of your physical and mental make-up. There are also views that place pleasure and pain in the context of historical changes in human cultures – so at one point in our cultural history something that is today found painful might at one point have been not painful at all. Here, we could more accurately be talking about suffering rather than pain. Historically, then, suffering was not in fact optional – at least if we use contemporary assessments of what we mean by suffering. In that respect, needing to grow or gather your food might be said to have involved more suffering than going to a store to buy it. Having to live without clean running water, either historically or in the contemporary world, would universally be regarded as suffering. These general explorations of pleasure and pain can be a guide to answering the question of what pleasure you personally gain from creative writing.

Creative writing, though it is not as physical an art as acting, dancing, or sculpting, for example, is similarly a process-based art, learnt and improved by practice, experiment, and repetition, and your physical acts of inscribing are what brings your creative and critical understanding to its impending written shape. Graham Fuller goes straight to process when interviewing English television dramatist, novelist, and journalist Dennis Potter on the pleasure Potter gains from creative writing:

> GF: *Do you still get pleasure out of the writing process?*
>
> DP: Yes, I do. I cuss it as well. Writing is difficult and directing is difficult, but then anything is difficult – playing a good game of football is difficult, isn't it?
>
> (Fuller, 1993: 141)

Creative writing being for Potter 'difficult' echoes the theme of suffering. Choose to write creatively, Potter says, and you choose to take on something that in order to be 'good' involves difficulty. We might wonder if difficulty always involves suffering or if, perhaps, we value and perhaps even seek out that which is difficult in celebration of the mind's control over the body.

Speaking to Daphne Kalotay for *The Paris Review*, short story writer and novelist Mavis Gallant adds yet a further twist. Nearing the end of her interview, Kalotay asks Gallant: 'Is writing generally an enjoyable experience?' Gallant replies: 'It's like a love affair: the beginning is the best part' (Kalotay, 1999: 195). The subtlety of Gallant's response is indicative of the quality also found in her fiction. Her writing is an 'affair' – by which she appears to suggest it is something she does not *expect* to be permanently satisfying; though, she suggests of course that it is intensely enjoyable at the outset. Not like love, then, but like a love *affair*, pleasurable, and yet … not leading or expecting to lead to happiness when undertaken at length.

The things you find pleasurable in creative writing are likely not all going to be agreeable to you. You will not find all of them enchanting. You might agree there is something of the theory of 'benign masochism' about this, or you might argue that theory fails to grasp how you actually go about your creative writing. For example, counter to that theory, you might not find the physical or mental undertaking of it threatening in the first place. Some of the pleasure in undertaking creative writing could come from the challenges it produces – creatively and intellectually. Wide evidence suggests pleasure is not all about comfortableness or coziness. Like the pleasure gained from sports, your pleasure in undertaking creative writing might be gained from empowerment, in such things as using words creatively, or telling a story, or presenting an image, or displaying an attitude or belief or understanding. Because such writing incorporates both the openness of creativity and the organizational necessities of written language use, the pleasure you derive from it can encompass the networking of cognitive and imaginative responses to life.

There are elements in the activity of creative writing that engage with play that incorporates both a personal sense of being able to express yourself and a sense too of social interaction, an invitation inherent in creative writing of contributing to a cultural and social world. There is the physical sensation of achievement, as one word is inscribed after the other, or whole sections of work completed, and the satisfaction gained from a labor undertaken and advanced or completed.

The Pleasures of 'Reading'

Some of your pleasure from creative writing comes from the pleasure you gain from reading. Reading is decoding with the aim of seeking meaning. The importance of first addressing reading in this broad way is that such an approach identifies reading as a natural and common aspect of human life. In that regard, when we in creative writing speak about reading we can productively begin by thinking of such common human activities as how we go about 'reading the weather or reading the tides' (Harper, 2013: 57). This consideration identifies reading as familiar and natural, part of being human, bringing attention to the fact that reading is not an arcane practice available only to some and it is not only associated with the reading (or writing) of texts.

Part of your pleasure as a creative writer is the heightened pleasure of investigating how and to what extent you are a reader, a decoder of what you experience in your immediate life as well as what you imagine. It is impossible to detach your writing and your reading because in your daily life you are indeed constantly reading. This has been so for humankind throughout time – because we have a curiosity, and are dependent on it, because the conditions of the world are not always obvious to us and the world constantly needs decoding, because we have social, cultural, and historical contexts that need understanding in order for us to act in commonsense ways, because to be *in* our lives we cannot only be passive receivers of sensory information we must be active interpreters, and because we have the intellectual and physical abilities to be makers of our lives.

Of course, as a creative writer you are reading to produce your creative works, to inform your day-to-day writerly actions, as well as to live in the world. Thinking of your pleasure in and from creative writing you can also consider the pleasure others gauge from reading or, thus defined, decoding your works. You can, just as significantly, consider yourself as your first reader – both in the process, as you shape a work or works, and as receiver when you consider these works complete. As a reader you draw on such skills as your ability to reason, making informed judgments, utilizing memories, having comprehension, and you can develop forms of literacy – cultural literacy, visual literacy, information literacy, media literacy, emotional literacy. Because we humans have created written texts we have also created a definition of literacy meaning the ability to understand and employ the signs and symbols we find in the writing of and the reading of texts. Some believe these specific, textually derived reading skills are of singular, conclusive importance in the practice of creative writing.

The Association of Writers and Writing Programs (AWP) says this on the section of its website entitled 'AWP Recommendations on the Teaching of Creative Writing to Undergraduates':

> An expert writer must first become an expert reader. The undergraduate creative writing curriculum seeks to inculcate an understanding of the rhetorical components, forms, genres, great works, and periods of literature. (AWP, 2017)

There is little doubt that familiarity with a genre or form can assist you in understanding what you are attempting to create. Informational, directional (in the manner of a signpost), perhaps imitative: completed examples provide guidance, augmenting your own compositional experience. Likewise, the historical context of works assists you in situating your contemporary activities, so that if indeed there are identifiable 'periods' of writerly work you can compare these with the one in which you are living. This said, if the

AWP is an organization concerned with creative writing, why is it that the focus here is on 'periods of literature' and 'great works'. Is creative writing only concerned with the creation of literature? In what sense do 'great works' define the day-to-day activities of creative writing and you as a creative writer? Are they exemplars applicable to the contemporary world in which you are writing? Perhaps. This all begins to create confusion, in that the AWP advice is clearly advertised as being about 'Teaching of Creative Writing'; but the pleasures of reading here are solely said to be about an approach to texts, and more about literature than any other kind of text:

> Creative writing classes and workshops introduce students to a wide range of literature, spanning at least three centuries, three continents, and a variety of cultural viewpoints. (AWP, 2017)

And further, surely suggesting something other than advice on the teaching and learning of creative writing is happening here:

> Workshops at all levels of a four-year course of study should require assigned texts: anthologies, novels, poetry collections, short story collections, nonfiction, and books on the craft of writing. Major and minor courses of study should include traditional classes in literature. (AWP, 2017)

This appears to be something to do with certain kinds of completed 'literature', in certain forms. 'Traditional' suggests classes related to the study of English perhaps. There are, nevertheless, 'books on the craft of writing'. Of course, because such activities as writing for film, the stage, music, new media are not mentioned there is further confusion as to what elements of the 'craft' of creative writing are actually being touted in the 'assigned texts' and why.

The pleasures of reading, like the pleasures of creative writing, are not limited to certain texts or indeed limited to texts at all. Coming to understand how those pleasures assist you in connecting with those in the world, interpreting, comprehending, and evaluating is a recognition of the eclecticism of creative writing, its inherent imaginative variety, and its enormous appeal. Some of the pleasures of reading, in that broad and imaginative context, include:

Decoding – Reading as actions making sense of the world around you and the entities formed in your imagination. You decoding these aspects offers a satisfying accomplishment, as well as providing a sense of organization where perhaps otherwise you would find disorder.

Engaging – Reading is a form of engagement, of active association making; while we might each enjoy time away from daily life, when we are within it to feel engaged, and be actively so, suggests you are part of a community, that you are a welcome inclusion in the habitat around you.

Acquiring (cognitive) – Reading is about acquisition, and on the level of personal value, the size of your inclusion in your own life and the lives of others, association with events, small and large, to acquire by reading, including the reading of your memories, is to positively increase your living 'footprint'.

Participating – Reading is active and therefore a participatory practice. Beyond the physical joy of such participation, the grasping of opportunity or the recognition of kinship, in the case of reading you are also actively deploying such enlivening aspects as the exploration of social affinities, the potential for collaborations, the responsiveness of that you perceive or imagine.

Personalizing – Your reading, while culturally informed and socially and historically influenced, is also profoundly personal. Therefore much about the pleasures of reading is also about the pleasure of being able to be yourself, sometimes ascertaining what that might be, seeking new knowledge about yourself through the reading of that beyond your literal and solo existence.

Because creative writing largely is regarded by us all as a welcome human activity, at times a valuable one and sometimes even a marvelous one, there is personal pleasure to be gained from doing something that is largely felt to be good. Even if the end results of your writing are not defined by critical or commercial opinion as exceptional, if your intentions are met the undertaking can still be pleasurable. There is further a sense of creative writing being an activity of bringing something into being, in this perhaps in creating the self as well as creating an object, the pleasure of declaration of your existence in the world. There is the pleasure of displaying knowledge or understanding, and a mode or modes of doing so that allows for considerable individualizing of this display. And there is the pleasure of being a reader of things, a reader who is actively engaged with the world, with others, with the imaginative, with the speculative, with what is real and what might be possible. None of this is to suggest that creative writing is without difficulty or without frustration or without elements from what Joyce Carol Oates has called 'the darker end of the spectrum' – but it could well be that how we understand the spectrum itself is more the question, rather than whether your attraction to creative writing reveals you have a dark side.

Exploring Pleasure

- Defining the pleasure you gain from creative writing is a personal undertaking that can move you closer to knowledge of what value you place in your writing. Not everything you include in that will be delightful – responses like 'challenging', 'demanding', 'tough', 'arduous' might be equally important to you as a creative writer.
- Suffering might indeed be optional; but because creative writing is both skill and knowledge, a physical practice and an imaginative/intellectual enterprise, a mode of communication and a form of art, it is not unexpected that moving from one way of comprehending and presenting ideas and feelings and other ways, endeavoring to traverse gaps between yourself and others, limited by the range of written language yet able to use that language in ways other writing forms do not encourage or support, all this suggests a degree of intensity, perhaps not best defined as 'suffering' but more accurately as 'convergence', and in creative writing that is not optional.

- The pleasure gained from the physical aspects of creative writing might not equal the happiness found by many in exercise, or produce the hormonal changes associated with such physiology of happiness, but physical pursuit of a goal, the sense of control that produces, the transferable vitality, the connection made between your feelings and thoughts, and the personal action, all that energizes you.
- You are also a reader, and to comprehend and apply what that means to your creative writing not only increases your pleasure in your reading and in your writing but also allows you to more fully employ a natural human propensity. Being a good reader, of texts certainly but also of other things, increases meaningfulness, and an increase in meaningfulness further and pleasurably situates us in our communities, our habitats, our personal experiences.
- A love of language appears to be a common trait among creative writers, with additional satisfaction gained from written language entailing a sense of longevity if not permanency.
- The empathetic nature of creative writing that you share through your works relates to how you experience the world with others and, however we define pleasure, how we create that shared sense of being.

Conclusion

Being a Creative Writer

Words and Action

'Desire' refers to a feeling that goes beyond a casual interest, and is far stronger than a passing thought. It is this to which Virginia Woolf refers when in a diary entry of Tuesday, August 17, 1937, she records the quickening conditions of her own writing: 'It's true, the only life this summer is in the brain. 3 hours pass like 10 minutes' (Bell, 1985: 107). And to which novelist and short story writer Gail Godwin refers in her diary entry of October 3, 1962:

> I have an idea, at last, about what I want to do. It is this: I want to say things on paper that will give expression to my own discoveries and at the same time make the reader richer in perception and enjoyment or awareness of his life.

> I want to experiment. I want to write the first things of their kind. (Godwin, 2006: 157)

A desire embeds itself in your sense of being, so that even if at first you do nothing to address that desire, the ache it creates, the thoughts it disrupts, the visions it produces persist and tempt and annoy and delight and will not, no matter how you might will it, wish it, or decide upon it, go away. That is what desire is.

In that respect, a desire to be a creative writer is no different than any other desire. If your desire is not strong enough, or if you concoct ways to ignore, dispel, or dilute that desire it will eventually diminish and potentially disappear. If it is not a desire at all, but is really a casual interest or a passing thought, then your creative writing won't happen or might happen but there is a very good chance that, if it does happen, it won't happen for very long. Creative writing is not so monotone, singular in complexion, or uncreative that a fleeting attraction to it is likely to produce a result with which you will be satisfied or that invigorates you so that you continue or that brings you pleasure, or that challenges you, or that connects your thoughts and your feelings, or that stimulates your aspirations to do more or become better at doing it. The title of this book, *The Desire to Write: The Five Keys to Creative Writing*, therefore refers to something quite specific. It does not refer to a situation in which you – reading here – have picked up this book to find out how to get this creative writing thing done apathetically. In other words, someone else might have written a book called *Very Little Desire to Write: The Keys to Not Having Much Interest in Creative Writing*, but this isn't that book.

However, your creative writing is also not predicated here on the notion that it always involves hard work, a great deal of difficulty, and some incredibly deep understanding of technical skills related to poetry, or fiction writing, or screenwriting, or playwriting, or the writing of any other type of creative writing, before you can even attempt to do it. In fact, if there is a message threaded throughout this book about the degree of work and the extent of your technical skills it is that your ways of working will be personal to you; that is, that they will be part of the story of *your* creative writing; that they will be learnt through informal means (that is, simply by writing creatively) and/or by formal means (that is, by undertaking some kind education in creative writing); and that what you need first and foremost to write creatively and to be a creative writer is a desire to write.

Inaction is by definition the death of your aspiration to be a creative writer. Creative writing fundamentally involves you taking action. Assuming that you do, this will bring about what can be called, as a guide, 'the event of creative writing', and this notion can work for one project or for all your projects. An event of creative writing will be informed by activities, thoughts, feeling, and observations that precede the event, laying the bedrock for it, as well as those that occur during the writing. The event of your creative writing will have a certain structure to it, and it will involve you or you and others, in the performance of the event, occur in episodes that are uncommon or are relatively common to your daily life, occur in an order, and last a certain amount of time. An example of an event of creative writing might be:

Your writing of a short story begins with you reading about an incident in history; you then imagine a character involved with that incident; you pose 'What if?' to consider an alternative episodic scenario; then do some preliminary note-taking, perhaps an attempt at an opening line or paragraph; a sudden burst of energy, next day, sees you finish three entire pages of the story; there's a moment where, while watching TV that evening, you revisit your 'What if?' question, drawing something from what you're watching; you write another page, unusually while doing something else that wasn't supposed to involve writing; an early morning walk has you deciding you should revise the now growing draft to make it occur in winter, when it's a little cold, like it is that morning; now, a sudden decision that the viewpoint is wrong; so you change it and start writing the story again; a moment, just as you wake, when you imagine the end of the story; a decision to focus more on a character that had been secondary at most until now; scrapping the opening few lines, you find the immediacy of entering the story more satisfying; you decide to set the story in the present rather than the past; the ending now seems wrong, so you change it; you finish a complete draft ... Perhaps now you're finished, perhaps you're not, not quite yet. Your event of creative writing has had an antecedent or antecedents, an origin, a duration, a pace, a structure, a set of episodes, some of which are familiar in your writing and some unique to this project (for example, you've never felt so strongly that a story should be set on a cold day as you are that *this* story should be set on a cold day), and these episodes have occurred in a particular order.

The impetus for your creative writing, or for any of your individual writing projects, might be an observation, or it might be a memory, or a feeling, or a number of feelings, or a combination of these things, or a combination of these things and other factors. No one stimulus is sure to impel your writing and none is absolutely destined to stop it or prevent it. Your creative writing will be supported by inspirations, motivations, and prompts, which might occur regularly and swiftly or might be infrequent or slow to occur, and might even make you consider that perhaps you won't complete the project you're working on – and sometimes you won't. Though creative writing involves an interaction between the imagination and intellect, and each has ways of assisting you to create and to conjecture and speculate, serendipity and fortuitousness will also play roles, and over these you will naturally have no control.

As you inscribe your writing, materially or virtually (on a screen, for one obvious example), using the tools of writing, or crafting, as a creative writer you are employing your imagination and your imagination is providing factual, counterfactual, or fantastical guidance; frequently, you are drawing on all three of these types of imagination. You make most progress with any activity of creative writing if something within it is familiar to you, or if your intentions in undertaking it are driven by your curiosity; and more so if your desire is matched by your determination to explore particular subjects or themes.

Harnessing the Elements

You begin by deciding what type of creative writing you are going to undertake. Will it be a poem, a short story, a novel, a screenplay, a work for the theater, or for a new form of media such as that seen in works of virtual reality? The choices of writing type are many, and some creative writers change their minds as a work progresses, deciding that what they thought was going to be one type of creative writing is not going to be that type at all. Both personal experience and personal preference, informed by your previous satisfaction as a creator or consumer of particular kinds of creative writing, drive your choice of creative writing type, and likewise inform your choice of genre and form. Exposure, education, and previous writing attempts energize your endeavors, and impact on your choices of type, genre, and form.

You make compositional choices as you write, these are singular (that is, 'actions'), and they form part of compositional collections of actions (that is, 'acts'). Your use of language sometimes favors the literal, sometimes incorporates the figurative. This language use is informed by the meeting of your intellect and your imagination, perhaps regularly also by your passion for language. Much as the overall event of creative writing contains many elements, so your compositional actions and acts contain singular occurrences and occurrences that are repeated and in that sense produce resonance in your compositional approach. You draft – that is, produce something for the first time, create raw material – and you revise – that is, return to drafted material and hone it, change it, sometimes you change it quite a bit – and you edit – that is, move your revised material toward a more conclusive shape, a final condition that you feel satisfies your intention.

Your intention or intentions should indeed be informing everything you are doing – for many creative writers, there are no intentions beyond our own, beyond those defined by each one of us, individually, whether those intentions are driven by a sense of who we are wanting to reach with our creative writing (for example, family, friends, a vast audience of largely unknown readers), or what we want to achieve with the final results of our creative writing (for example, financial gain, communicating our ideas, our feelings, a theme or subject for which we have a particular passion). For some creative writers, the intention or intentions are set by others (for example, when the results have a purpose defined by a teacher, or set in motion by a commercial contract). Your intentions are supported by such things as your commitment (quite simply, to the labor involved), perhaps some planning (either or both physical and/or mental preparation), some form of reasoning (that is, while emotional engagement might inspire you, writing involves reasoned behaviors; emotion alone cannot produce creative writing), and your perceptions (of why creative writing is a good thing to do, and of why you intend to do it).

As you write creatively, you are having such experiences as discovering and exploring newness; shifting planes of reference; pursuing curiosity; creating representations that illustrate and bring an idea, an emotion, to life; involvement in play (which includes spontaneity and a sense of performing); determining and constructing meaning; and, not least because writing is for communication, interacting with others, even if those others are imaginary, not physically present.

All creative writing involves structures, forms, functions, and systems. That is, the kinds of apparatus associated with language and, specifically, with written language. But it is the creative that is making it distinctive as you write, empowering the visual and aural imaginings you have, the mental representations you create, the concepts drawn from memory, supposition, conjecture, and speculation.

Some aspects you employ are complex, others are simple. In your creative writing, you categorize and organize, create sequences and relationships between what, why, and who. All this is drawn from and influenced by your personal psychology and your social and cultural background.

You, Creative Writer

In the Introduction I provided three examples of creative writers – a school student, a professor, and a hospital patient – to make the point that anyone can be a creative writer. Though the image of the creative writer, over time, has sometimes suggested that a creative writer has a certain take on the world, a particular set of character traits, a certain outlook, this is more romance than it is reality. Creative writing most certainly involves technical writing skills, but feeling, belief, motivation are at least as important as those skills. We might even say that such technical skills can be learnt, but feeling, belief, and motivation cannot. If you have a desire to write creatively, and if you refuse to ignore, dispel, or dilute that desire, then you can write creatively.

You have a desire to write for a reason. That reason is mostly likely supported by emotional engagement, and your wish to pursue creative writing for some purpose, to gain some kind of satisfaction, maybe not all pleasure in a narrow sense of the term, but certainly satisfaction. You will have individual motivation and that motivation will empower a pattern of behavior, the physical practice, the nature of your expressiveness, the empathy you imbue in your work, the changing of the ordinary communicative

Conclusion

function of written language to an extraordinary use, even an inspired use. You will decode language, in order to use it; engage with and acquire ideas and feelings; participate in as much as mold the work you are creating, imaginatively; and personalize the practice and its results so that when you feel your project is complete that feeling will be as much an individual sense as it is a sense of it being time to release your work to a reader or audience. The five keys explored in this book – intention, action, emotion, imagination, and pleasure – will guide you in any creative writing you do, and form the basis on which your writing skills can be employed, and develop, and truly support that wonderful ambition you have: the desire to write.

Notes

Introduction: So You Want to be a Creative Writer?

Josephine Humphreys, 'Perfect Family Self-Destructs: Review of Ordinary Love and Good Will, Two Novellas by Jane Smiley', *New York Times Book Review*, November 5, 1989.

Chapter 1: Intention

Neil Gaiman, *Fragile Things: Short Fictions and Wonder*, New York: Harper Collins, 2007.
Mario Vargas Llosa, *A Writer's Reality*, London: Faber, 1991.
Christopher D. Morris, ed., *Conversations with E.L. Doctorow*, Jackson: University of Mississippi Press, 1999.
R. Keith Sawyer, 'Writing as a Collaborative Act' in Scott Barry Kaufmann and James C. Kaufmann (eds), *The Psychology of Creative Writing*, New York: Cambridge University Press, 2009.

Chapter 2: Action

Nancy Topping Bazin and Marilyn Dallman Seymour, *Conversations with Nadine Gordimer*, Jackson: University of Mississippi Press, 1990.

Mari Evans, ed., *Black Women Writers: Arguments and Interviews*, London: Pluto Press, 1985.

Giles Gordon, ed., 'Alan Burns' in *Beyond Words: Eleven Writers in Search of New Fiction*, London: Hutchinson, 1975.

Nick Holt, *The Wit and Wisdom of Great Writers*, King's Sutton: House of Raven, 2006.

Christina Kallas, 'Warren Leight (In Treatment, Lights Out, Law & Order: Special Victims Unit)' in *Inside the Writers' Room: Conversations with American TV Writers*, New York: Palgrave Macmillan, 2014.

Larry W. Phillips, ed., *F. Scott Fitzgerald On Writing*, Wellingborough: Equation, 1988.

George Plimpton, ed., 'Philip Roth', in *Writers at Work: The Paris Review Interviews*, New York: Viking, 1986.

Jacob Shamsian, 'Here's How Long It Took to Write 30 of the Most Famous Books in the World', *Business Insider*, September 2, 2016, http://www.businessinsider.com/how-long-it-takes-to-write-a-book-2016-9 (last accessed June 10, 2018).

Chapter 3: Emotion

John Barth, *Further Fridays: Essays, Lectures and Other Non-Fiction, 1984–1994*, Boston: Little Brown, 1995.

Daniel Goleman, *Emotional Intelligence: Why It Can Matter More Than IQ*, New York: Bantam Books, 1995.

Nick Holt, *The Wit and Wisdom of Great Writers*, King's Sutton: House of Raven, 2006.

Stephen Jay Gould, *The Mismeasure of Man*. New York: W. W. Norton & Company, 1981.

Immanuel Kant, *Critique of Judgement*, Translated by James Creed Meredith, Oxford: Oxford University Press, 2007 (original publication date 1952).

Vladimir Nabokov, 'Good Readers and Good Writers' in Fredson Bowers (ed.), *Vladimir Nabokov, Lectures on Literature*, New York: Harvest, 1980.

Joyce Carol Oates, *The Faith of the Writer: Life, Craft, Art*, New York: HarperCollins, 2003.

Chapter 4: Imagination

Ruth Byrne, *The Rational Imagination: How People Create Alternatives to Reality*, Cambridge, MA: MIT Press, 2005.

Ruth Byrne, 'Precis of the Rational Imagination: How People Create Alternatives to Reality', *Behavioral and Brain Sciences*, vol. 30, no. 5–6, 2007, pp. 439–480.

William Gass, *Finding a Form: Essays by William Gass*, Ithaca, NY: Cornell University Press, 1996.

Günter Grass, *On Writing and Politics: 1967–1983*, New York: Harcourt, 1985.

Colin McGinn, *Mindsight: Image, Dream, Meaning*, Cambridge, MA: Harvard University Press, 2004.

Jean-Paul Sartre, *Words*, London: Penguin, 1967.

Chapter 5: Pleasure

AWP (Association of Writers and Writing Programs), 'AWP Recommendations on the Teaching of Creative Writing to Undergraduates', AWP, https://www.awpwriter.org/guide/

directors_handbook_recommendations_on_the_teaching_of_creative_writing_to_undergraduates (last accessed August 20, 2017).

Graham Fuller, ed., *Potter on Potter (Directors on Directors)*, Faber: London, 1993.

Graeme Harper, 'Creative Writing Habitats' in Dianne Donnelly and Graeme Harper (eds), *Key Issues in Creative Writing*, Bristol: Multilingual Matters, 2013.

Daphne Kalotay, 'Mavis Gallant, The Art of Fiction, No.160', *Paris Review*, Issue 153, Winter 1999, pp. 192–211.

Haruki Murakami, *What I Talk About When I Talk About Running*, New York: Vintage, 2008.

Joyce Carol Oates, *The Faith of a Writer: Life, Craft and Art*, New York: Harper Collins, 2004.

Paul Rozin, Lily Guillot, Katrina Fincher, Alexander Rozin, and Eli Tsukayama, 'Glad to Be Sad, and Other Examples of Benign Masochism', *Judgment and Decision Making*, Vol. 8, No. 4, July 2013, pp. 439–447.

Conclusion: Being a Creative Writer

Anne Olivier Bell, *The Diary of Virginia Woolf, Volume 5: 1936–1941*, London: Penguin, 1985.

Gail Godwin, *The Making of a Writer: Journals 1961–1963*, New York: Random House, 2006.

Index

Acquiring   111
Acts   44–49, 64, 120
Aspirations   28, 116
Association of Writers and Writing Programs (AWP)   109–110, 127

Barth, John   66
Belief   ix, 56–57, 68, 82, 100, 103, 107, 122
Blake, William   x

Commitment   3–4, 7, 10, 22, 24, 25, 121
Compositional questions   7–25, 120
Connectivity   32, 85, 91
Counterfactual Imagination   71, 74, 75–76, 84, 119
Craft   66, 67, 82
Creative Imagination   71, 74
Critique of Judgement   61

Cultural significance   101–102
Curiosity   84–85, 108

Decoding   107, 108, 111
Dillard, Annie   33
Doctorow, E. L.,   22
Drafting   24, 41, 47
Duration   38–39, 42, 118

Editing   4, 24, 47, 120
Emotional Intelligence   62–63, 64
Emotive   59, 63, 64–66, 68
Empathy   62, 68, 100–102, 122
Enactment   40, 48
Engagement   46, 76, 82, 83, 88, 111, 121
Event   18, 19, 34, 35–44, 46, 48, 49, 56, 63, 64, 117
Experiences   11, 13
Expressiveness   99, 103, 122

129

Factual Imagination 71, 74, 75, 77, 78, 81, 84, 92, 119
Feelings 22, 24, 31, 34, 35, 40, 44–46, 51, 54–56, 61–65, 68
Figuration 90–91
Fitzgerald, F. Scott 41
Form 8, 18–22

Gaiman, Neil 2–3
Gallant, Mavis 106
Gass, William 76
Genre 8, 15–18, 19, 30, 35, 38, 48, 56, 109, 120
Godwin, Gail 115
Gordimer, Nadine 36–37
Grass, Günter 89

Habitat 22–24, 111, 114

Imagination
  See Factual Imagination; Creative Imagination; Counterfactual Imagination
Inaction 27, 28, 30, 32, 117
Inscribing 27, 65, 98, 119
Interaction 23, 37, 68, 91–92, 100

Language ix, 5, 6, 12, 18, 31, 37, 59, 61, 65, 67, 77, 83, 99–100, 113
Libretto 10
Llosa, Mario Vargas 12

Memory 35, 58, 77, 85, 89, 121
Mental representations x, 72, 77–83, 121
Metaphor 33, 45, 76, 81, 87–88
Mills and Boon 51–54
Motivation 51, 57–59, 85, 122
Murakami, Haruki 96

Nabokov, Vladimir 55
Newness 59, 85–87, 93
Nin, Anaïs 35
Novel 4, 11, 14, 51, 96

Occupational category xix–xx, 29
Order 40, 42, 48
Ordinary-Extraordinary 102

Pain 96, 103, 104, 105
Participation 41–44, 48, 102, 112

Patterns   13, 22–25, 34, 39
Perception   6–7, 10, 24, 54, 58, 72, 73, 88, 100, 121
Personalizing   112, 123
Physicality   5, 6, 11, 14, 22, 23, 27, 33, 36, 42, 46, 52, 59, 87, 88, 96, 98–99, 103, 104, 105, 107, 112, 113, 114, 121
Planes of reference   87–88, 121
Planning   4–5, 24, 47
Play   89–90
Poetry   xv–xvi, 9, 21, 38, 48, 60
Potter, Dennis   106

Reading   5–6, 107–113
Reasoning   x, 6, 19, 24, 38, 103, 121
Revising   24, 47, 64
Rilke, Rainer Maria   97–98
Roth, Philip   48

Sartre, Jean-Paul   83
Screenplay   9, 10, 21
Self-confidence   4, 34
Smiley, Jane   x
Span   39
Structure   37–38, 68, 81, 92, 121
Success   13, 14, 25, 35, 60, 61, 64, 101
Suffering   95–97, 103, 106, 113
Synapses   32, 34, 100

Type   8–15, 19, 28, 60, 93, 119

Value   16, 65, 66, 69, 111, 113

Waugh, Evelyn   57
Woolf, Virginia   115–116
'Writer's block'   32

Printed by Printforce, the Netherlands